Sincerely, Andy Rooney

Sincerely, Andy Rooney

Andy Rooney

PublicAffairs
NEW YORK

Published in the United States by PublicAffairs™,
a member of the Perseus Books Group.

Printed in the United States of America.

Book design by Jenny Dossin.

Illustration of Andy Rooney's Underwood typewriter
copyright © 1999 by John MacDonald.

LIBRARY OF CONGRESS CATALOGING-IN-PUBLICATION DATA
Rooney, Andrew A.
Sincerely, Andy Rooney / Andy Rooney.—1st ed.
p. cm.
ISBN 1-891620-34-7
1. Rooney, Andrew A.—Correspondence. 2. Humorist—United States—Correspondence. I. Title.
PN6162 .R6333 1999
816'.54 21—dc21

99-043726

FIRST EDITION

1 3 5 7 9 10 8 6 4 2

CONTENTS

PREFACE

ONE OF THE GOOD THINGS in life is getting a personal letter. Not many come in the mail anymore. They've been replaced by the telephone, the form letter and now, email. Too bad. There are not many little pleasures better than going to the mailbox and finding a real letter from a friend.

Most of the letters in this book were written in response to ones sent to me by readers or viewers who liked, disliked or had a comment to make about something I wrote in my newspaper column or said on television. Others are friendly letters to friends, angry letters to government functionaries or representatives of a business with which I've had some dealing—usually an unsatisfactory one.

There are a lot of letters having to do with my work as a writer for newspapers, magazines and television. I have worked for every president CBS News ever had.

While it was not my intention when I started this, I realized halfway through that I was writing—or assembling—a sort of striated autobiography. There's a lot of my life in this book but I say "striated" because there are whole strains of it that don't come up here because I never wrote letters about them. Still, a great many of the thoughts I've ever had about almost everything come up somewhere in a letter I wrote. They're here.

You don't need a detailed chronicle of events in a person's life to know almost everything about him. The smallest things we do often give away our whole character. We can't get away from being ourselves or sounding like ourselves all day long, all life long. Whatever we do, we do it the same way we did the last thing we did. The same things keep happening, good and bad, to the same people all their lives because of what they are like and how they do things.

After reading some of the letters I've written, I think less of myself than I did before. I have frequently been dumb, sometimes unnecessarily nasty or negative. Reading these letters, I've been an unpleasant surprise to myself sometimes and may be to you. On the other hand, if I don't come off as nice, I sound basically decent and, as far as my intellect goes, intellectually honest.

In my own view of myself, I am normal beyond the ability of anyone who knows me only as a public figure to believe. I am a middle-of-the-road, average, everyday American. I'm so normal and average (and normal, average people are so rare) that I'm practically one of a kind.

My life has divided itself into five major sections—childhood, school and college, World War II, marriage and a family and my work as a writer. I have a big appetite for both food and life and each of those divisions has been so satiating that I could not say which of them has been best, happiest or most satisfying. They have all been those things.

This book often concerns itself with things that came about as a result of my work as a writer, including those parts of my writing I did as a reporter for the Army newspaper, *The Stars and Stripes*, between 1942 and 1945. That war was an incredible experience, many of the details of which won't go away. Sometimes I can't keep myself from repeating them even though I know that people who weren't there may be bored by them. I wrote hundreds of articles for the paper and almost daily I receive mail from someone who has been rummaging around the attic and came on a story I wrote about him or his unit. He wants to share it with me.

My childhood and youth was ecstatically happy. I've often thought I might have been a better writer if I had lived a tortured, miserably unhappy early life but I didn't and I haven't said much about that here.

Considering what a major part of my life my family has been, it doesn't come up much, either. You don't write letters to people you see every day.

A person is much less guarded about what he writes in a letter than what he says in public and there are a lot of unguarded comments I've made in these letters. There are some little bombs that may go off and I'm not sure which letters will cause the explosions. I'm doing this anyway—putting the letters in print anyway—because it's satisfying fun.

Over the years, on television and in articles for print, I have curbed myself from writing and saying some of the things that are in these letters. You have to choose your causes in public because you can't fight a battle on every front. My manner of dress is an example of that. I don't like neckties but I wear a necktie because I'm not interested in taking a stand there. Neckties are not a battle I want to fight. It often saves time to blend in with the crowd. I have never said much about religion or even politics because I wanted to blend in but I do say things about both of them here.

All the letters in this book were written by me. When someone writes a letter, the words remain the property of the person who put them down on paper. The paper itself belongs to the person the letter was sent to. For this reason, and because I have no interest in being really fair, I have not included letters written by anyone else in this book. Joyce Maynard sold the fourteen love letters written to her by the reclusive J.D. Salinger but, while she could sell the paper they were written on, she could not have included Salinger's words to her in a book without his permission.

Having almost no words but my own in the book gives me an advantage over the letter writers. I always win because there is no rebuttal and, except occasionally where I have paraphrased their point as an introduction to my own letter, they don't even get to present their original argument. My position is "Let them write their own book."

I have taken liberties with some of my original letters, editing many of them and even making a few word changes where it should have been said better or quicker in the first place. For an example, I often begin a letter with something like "Thank you for writing" or "I enjoyed your good letter." I took all of those out. I edited out whole paragraphs where they were too personal and had nothing to do with the basic point of the letter.

Saving a copy of a letter you've written is not a sign of humility but in most cases the letters I wrote and saved copies of were not so much ego as accident, the efficiency of an assistant or a matter of technology. Jane Bradford worked with me for years and she kept the original letters sent to me and copies of the ones I wrote in reply. After about 1989, when I started using a computer full time, I automatically stored away the letters I wrote on my hard drive. Susan Bieber, who works with me, did a lot of sorting things out.

I have removed such unnecessary details as dates, addresses and formal closings to my letters where they have no bearing on the content. The names of some of the people I wrote to are often without any further identification because I don't have any and where dates were of no significance, I've left those out.

Geoff Shandler is no doubt handsomely paid as chief among editors at PublicAffairs but I thank him in addition for his good work and for throwing out some letters I liked. Kate Darnton threw out some letters I liked, too. When anyone edited anything that Fred Allen wrote, he said "Where were they when the paper was blank?"

Peter Osnos, the publisher at PublicAffairs, decided to do this book but you don't thank publishers because it can only make things worse.

PART ONE

My Government, My Money

There was no logical order in which to assemble this disorderly book. It has not been laid out chronologically and, while there may be a logical place to end it, there was no obvious beginning. Starting it will be more like opening your refrigerator door.

I've always had a special talent for bookkeeping and financial transactions.

Lost Securities
First Chicago Trust Company of New York
SBC Communications, Inc.
Box 2506, Jersey City, New Jersey

I am missing 1700 shares of Exxon stock bought in May 1986. The certificate, issued 7/22/86 according to the broker's record, was number 648912.

I don't know whether or not the circumstances matter but I am certain that the stock was simply misplaced and is somewhere in my possession. It has been missing since I moved my office with hundreds of boxes, books and files four years ago.

Could you please advise me on how to proceed and what the procedure will cost? I am also missing an explanation of why your company is called The First Chicago Trust Company of New York in Jersey City.

Mr. Art Semione
Tax Technician II
New York State Department of Taxation and Finance

Dear Mr. Semione,

Today I received your letter asking for more information, which you want in a hurry, about my 1987 New York State income tax . . . which I filed 210 days ago.

As a resident of Connecticut and frequent traveler, I filed for a rebate for tax deducted from my paycheck for days I worked out of New York State. That payment is still due me.

Your letter poses four questions.

You ask, for instance, for "the exact location where your services were performed and the nature of the services performed at each location."

This is a tough question for a writer to answer in a way that might satisfy a Tax Technician, Mr. Semione. You see, a writer is often working even when he isn't typing and the "nature" of his work is a little vague.

I don't know how to say this to a Tax Technician in a way that won't sound silly to him but sometimes a writer only watches. It probably wouldn't seem to a lot of people as though a person was working when he was merely watching but that's the way a writer works.

Years ago, a good writer named Morley Callaghan said "There is only one trait that marks the writer. He is always watching. It's a kind of trick of mind and a writer is born with it."

In view of this, how exact do you want me to be about the location and nature of my work? If I answered that question by saying "Watching in Philadelphia" would that be exact enough?

To be honest with you, Art—can I call you Art?—I wander a lot when I'm working and wandering is just the opposite from being at an "exact location." I'm almost certain you wouldn't accept "Watching and

Wandering outside New York" for the nature of my work and its exact location but that's the truth of it.

No days "worked at home" were included in my days worked outside NYS because, while I did actually work at home for my company on at least ten days of the year, I know that it is considered a suspicious activity by you IRS people so I thought it wise not to claim them. I worked at home on some of those days because the railroad I use to get to work on in New York was shut down and getting to work would have taken more time than my work was worth.

On other days I worked at home because it was the efficient thing to do under the circumstances although I use the word "efficient" reluctantly because when it comes to efficiency I rank right alongside your Department of Taxation and Finance.

Your question #4 asks for "the date of each non-working day other than Saturdays and Sundays." I take exception to your always excluding Saturdays and Sundays from the work week. We are not all government workers. I do some of my best work Sundays.

You're welcome to come to my home and see the work areas I have. There are eight file cabinets, several hundred reference books, seventeen typewriters and two computers in my office.

In conclusion, let me ask *you* four questions:

1. Your letter came the day the newspapers carried the story saying New York State is two billion dollars over budget. Is New York State trying to help make up that deficit by being deliberately slow in paying me what it owes?

2. How much interest has the State made on the money it owes me?

3. You ask that I reply "within 20 days so that this matter may be handled promptly." Having delayed handling this matter for seven months, why is the State tax department now in such a hurry?

4. Could you tell me what the average payment is for someone in my

tax bracket and also whether anyone in my tax bracket paid more taxes than I did? Just a general statement. I wouldn't ask you for names.

If you come to my home to see my office there, bring your own coffee because I wouldn't want to be accused of trying to bribe a tax agent with a cup of that.

And, if it is in your power, please issue orders for me to be paid the amount due me within five days . . . to ensure that this matter is handled promptly.

Andrew Rooney
Taxpayer

. . .

Mr. James SQRX QXZinn,
District Director
Hartford District
Internal Revenue Service

Dear Mr. X,

Because your name is illegible as signed in your form letter to me dated February 8, 1999, and because you failed to provide me with a legible, typed name I am unable to address you properly. I assume the signature was made illegible intentionally to preclude your getting angry letters from taxpayers like myself. I would like to have sat in at the meeting in your office when the decision was made to obscure your signature. It accurately reflects the inept arrogance with which my case was handled by your Norwalk office.

James E. Quinn
Internal Revenue Service
Hartford, Connecticut

Dear Mr. Quinn,

Thank you for your restrained response to my testy letter. I did talk with Edward Connelly, of your Norwalk office, on the phone and told him I'd come up with something more in a month. I have not done that because I don't know what to come up with.

The matter is further complicated because New York State is also after me, charging that I'm a resident of that State. I am not. If I were a resident of both New York and Connecticut, I should have the right to vote in both States. Could you arrange that for me?

. . .

Thomas D. Ritter
House of Representatives
Hartford, Connecticut

Dear Mr. Ritter,

Thank you for your invitation to visit the State Capitol Building. There are a great many things I'd like to do and can't find time for and that's one of them. Having a reception there in my honor is a terrible idea. I'm at my worst at receptions for me.

It was nice to be put in a category of "notable Connecticut residents" but you should know that, in the eyes of New York State, I'm not a resident of Connecticut but of New York. I worked more than 183 days in New York in 1991 and anyone who does that is a resident on their books. I am not a resident of New York, of course. We've lived in the same house in Connecticut since 1951 and raised a family there. I pay Connecticut taxes but New York doesn't care about details. Can they tax me without allowing me to vote? I'm going to register to vote in New York next year with a Connecticut address and see what happens. I plan to vote in Connecticut, too.

Having paid my 1994 taxes on time after preparing it with the help of a good accountant who doesn't fudge the numbers, I was angered to get another letter signed by James E. Quinn, my IRS District Director.

"We selected your Federal Income Tax return for the year shown below for review to examine the items listed at the end of this letter" he wrote.

I went to the end of the letter to see what they wanted to examine. Among other items listed was:

"JOB-HUNTING EXPENSES"

"Log or diary showing job-hunting activity, and cancelled checks or receipts showing expenses paid for this activity, including payments to employment agencies."

. . .

Dear Mr. Quinn,

Before I come in for the review you demand, let me ask you some questions:

1. Does someone in as responsible a job as you have send out letters over his signature without reading them?

2. Are you reviewing a lot of returns needlessly to provide people in your office with work because you have more people working for you than you need?

3. When you signed the letter to me, did you look at my tax return before you decided to put me to all the trouble and angst of preparing for a review?

4. Did you see how much money I made last year? Did you note that at my age I get a pension from the Writers' Guild, the American Federation of Radio and Television Artists and from Essay Productions? Did you see where I get $13,000 in Social Security? Did you know I've worked for the same company since 1949 and still work there? Do you ever watch television? Do you know I am well paid for doing a regular piece on one of the most popular shows? Do you read your local paper and note that they carry this column along with 150 other papers in the Country, each one of which pays me money? Have you ever read a book? I spent long hours writing my World War II memoir that's in bookstores now and for which the publisher paid me a handsome advance.

In view of all this, Mr. Quinn, how much time, money and effort do you think I spent looking for work or, as you say "job-hunting?" Do you really think I listed my name with an employment agency? Have you ever thought of looking for another job yourself?

The last item you want me to justify is "UNIFORMS, EQUIPMENT, AND TOOLS." You ask for "a description of the item."

It surprises me that you didn't already know this, Mr. Quinn, because I listed my occupation as "writer." Writers do not wear uniforms. I've known a lot of them and I don't think I ever recall seeing a writer in any kind of a uniform unless you call baggy corduroys and an L.L. Bean blue denim shirt a uniform. I wear those a lot but if you'll take the trouble of actually looking at my tax return, you'll see that I didn't even take the prorated cost of wear-and-tear on my ten-year old corduroys.

As for equipment, I don't remember what I put in for on my tax form and I don't have it on hand here, but it couldn't have been much. I have seventeen old Underwood #5 typewriters and, while I only use a couple of them, I think I have enough to last me to the end of my writing life so I won't be asking for a tax deduction there for "equipment."

I use a computer a lot now but I've had mine for several years and I don't think I applied for much of any equipment deduction. Maybe a few typewriter ribbons.

You ask about tools. I did get a new, very small, screwdriver to fix the handle on my laptop but that's all I can think of and I doubt if I put in for that screwdriver.

My basic question to you is this, Mr. Quinn, and I'd like an answer within ten days: Are the people in your IRS office stupid, inefficient or did someone there think it would be fun to have Andy Rooney come in so they could get his autograph?

Do you understand, Mr. Quinn, that sexual is not the only form of harassment?

. . .

E.B. Gurewitz
Dept. of Taxation & Finance
New York, New York

Dear Mr. Gurewitz,

This is to confirm our tax review date for January 7th, 1993.

I received your request asking me to sign an extension beyond the April 15, 1993 limit. This suggests you are busier than I am. It seems to me as though there's ample time to resolve this in the more than four months left before the statutory limit expires. I certainly would like to have it off my mind before then and I could be available at any time.

I was gratified to note that the person from your office who wrote the consent request letter is as bad with language as I am with numbers. Some of it borders on being illiterate. For example, this sentence: "Since failure to receive these Consent forms timely automatically results in the issuance of an assessment for tax due, plus penalty and interest, please be sure that the forms are completed properly and mailed promptly."

I thought we had resolved most of the issues at our first meeting. There is something wrong about any citizen paying taxes to both New York State and Connecticut unless he can vote in two States. I should pay non-resident taxes on my New York State income to New York. Tax on other income on work done in Connecticut where, for example, I write my newspaper column, should be paid to Connecticut. I am indeed, a resident of Connecticut, not New York. My doctor, my dentist, my stores are in Connecticut. I have a Connecticut driver's license. I vote there. I do not live in New York even though I spend several days a week working there.

. . .

June 2, 1999

Julianne Martinez
Chase Visa
Fraud Operations

Dear Ms. Martinez,

Your letter dated May 21, calling for my prompt attention to a possible fraudulent use of my Visa card, was postmarked May 24 and delivered June 2nd.

I will give it my prompt attention sometime soon.

PART TWO

A Funny Business

The world is divided between people who keep stuff and people who throw it out. I keep it.

For what reason I don't know but immediately after World War II, Communism appealed to a great many bright American intellectuals—there are dumb intellectuals.

Some of my friends from The Stars and Stripes and YANK magazine met regularly at Tim Costello's bar on Third Avenue in New York and were trying to organize to get Henry Wallace, the most liberal of the candidates, elected President. I went to Costello's occasionally and was surprised to find, later, that some of my friends had actually joined the American Communist Party. It didn't seem terrible to me, just dumb.

Later, when I worked at MGM in Hollywood, I made friends with a man named Lester Cole. He was one of their best screenwriters. I liked him and we had lunch together frequently and dinner occasionally. I don't ever recall talking politics or economics with Lester.

He invited us to an anti-Franco fund-raising dinner for what was called "the Barsovie Hospital" which I understood to be somewhere in the Basque region of Spain where wounded Spanish freedom-fighters were treated. We sat at a table in the banquet room and when the master of ceremonies started pointing at tables to ask how much we'd give, I didn't want to call attention to myself by being the only piker in the crowd and offered a table-low of $25.

It was months before I knew "the Barsovie Hospital" dinner was a Communist Party event. For some reason my name never surfaced and the $25 didn't buy me entrée to any list of "subversives."

By the time I went to work for Arthur Godfrey at CBS, in 1949, Senator Joseph McCarthy was on a vicious campaign to purge the news and entertainment business in both Hollywood and New York of all its communist, socialist or left-leaning members. A serious Democrat could easily have been swept up by McCarthy's broad broom and I was lucky it missed that $25 check of mine and my friendship with Lester Cole because Lester had been sent to prison as one of "The Hollywood Ten."

A great many Americans approved of McCarthy but a great many detested everything about his campaign. Unfortunately, even some of those who hated it knuckled under and submitted to McCarthy because they were afraid. He could ruin a person or a company by merely suggesting a communist connection. Executives of the Columbia Broadcasting System did not distinguish themselves in this regard.

Dr. Frank Stanton has been the object of a lot of criticism for his part in the corporate cave-in. While I know nothing about the part he played, he may have made a mistake. If he did, he more than made up for it in his subsequent years as president of the company with his brilliant and courageous defense of the network's First Amendment rights.

One of the things I never threw away is a collector's item today. It is the original memo from a CBS executive asking CBS employees to sign the non-communist oath.

Columbia Broadcasting System, Inc.
OFFICE COMMUNICATION
December 19, 1950

To: The Organization
From: Joseph Ream

In the last war, radio, and CBS, played a vital and important role. In some areas of our operations—short wave programming and transmitter operation, and laboratory developmental work—were under direct contract with the federal government. The value of broadcasting's contribution has been attested by high government officials and, even more significantly, by the many millions of listeners who depended on radio for information, inspiration and entertainment during the period of crisis.

Today, we are faced with a new crisis in our national life. The President of the United States has declared a national emergency. If we are to fulfill our obligations and responsibilities as radio and television broadcasters in this new crisis, we must do at least two things: First, we must make sure that our broadcasting operations in the public interest are not interrupted by sabotage or violence; second, we must make sure that the full confidence of our listeners and viewers is unimpaired.

To accomplish the first objective we will institute measures for physical security generally similar to those existing in the last war.

To accomplish the second objective we are asking each employee to answer the questions on the form attached, which we will keep confidential, unless at some future time the information is demanded by a governmental security agency. These questions are *identical* to those appearing in the Civil Service Commission application for federal government.

Because of the unique nature of broadcasting, it is most important that, for the good of both the country and our own organization, there be no question concerning loyalty to our country of any CBS employee. We are all aware that in the past year certain groups have raised questions concerning alleged subversive influences in broadcasting. It is important that the true facts—based on the statement of each employee—be established.

J. H. R.

Note: Please return signed questionnaire to your department head or, if you prefer, direct to my office.

The questionnaire asked each of us to swear we were not now and never had been members of the Communist Party and had never worked for anyone who was.

My response to Ream's memo was a tortured attempt on my part to be funny by parodying his memo.

To: Mr. Joseph H. Ream, Columbia Broadcasting System
From: Andrew A. Rooney

In the last war, I played a small unimportant role. I was for four years a soldier in the United States Army.

Today we face a new crisis. The President of the United States has declared a National Emergency.

If I am once again to fulfill my obligations as a citizen of this free democracy, I must do at least two things: First, I must try to maintain my personal liberty; second, to continue to enjoy the pursuit of happiness (and what of it I catch), I must continue to be employed for the satisfaction of having an outlet for my work and for the income which supports my wife, self and three children.

To accomplish both these objectives, I am signing the memorandum which I first received on February 2, 1951, and in return I am asking that I be sent a statement to the effect that neither the chairman of the board, William S. Paley, nor the president of the Columbia Broadcasting System, Frank Stanton, is now or ever has been, a member of the Communist Party or any of the organizations listed as totalitarian, fascist or communist or subversive by the Attorney General of the United States.

The only good sense I showed was in not sending that memo and neither did I return the questionnaire with my signature.

Several weeks later I got a second memo from another CBS executive.

Columbia Broadcasting System, Inc.
OFFICE COMMUNICATION

January 29, 1951

TO: CBS contract personnel
FROM: Gerald F. Maulsby

On December 19, 1950, the attached memorandum and statement for signature were distributed to all CBS payroll employees and contract personnel.

As it is possible a copy may not have reached you, this further one is now being forwarded to your attention. After it has been checked and signed, will you please return it to the office of Joseph H. Ream, Executive Vice-President.

Many thanks.
G.F.M.

For many years, when I had been asked if I had signed the non-communist oath at CBS during the blacklisting scandal, I had told people that I had refused. It turns out I was not so brave as my memory of myself.

I wrote a second memo which I did send and did sign.

TO: Gerald Maulsby
FROM: Andrew A. Rooney

I have signed and am returning the so-called "non-communist oath" paper which I first received December 21, 1951 from Joseph Ream. I assume there will be made available to me a statement to the effect that neither the chairman of the board, William S. Paley nor the president of the Columbia Broadcasting System, Dr. Frank Stanton, is now or ever has been a member of the Communist Party or any of the organizations listed as totalitarian, fascist, communist or subversive listed by the Attorney General of the United States.

I never got the statement I asked for attesting to the fact that neither Paley nor Stanton were communists.

. . .

August 25, 1950

David Klinger
CBS Business Affairs

Dear Dave,

Charley Slocum and I have never read the contract we signed last year to write the Talent Scout show for Arthur Godfrey. Contracts are not designed to be read by writers.

I think it ran for two years but it may have been life. If it was for life, I don't know whether it was for my life or the life of the show, whichever is longer.

Neither of us honestly believe Arthur would be back in Baltimore selling birdseed without us, but we thought we did a good job of writing last year for both Arthur and Cedric Adams the night he stood in when Arthur was away. We were paid $150 a week each. The show was the #1 rated show on television for nine weeks last year and always in the top five.

Charley and I thought it would be best to make a direct approach, without going through the Guild or an agent, and simply ask for more money.

I know little or nothing about who has anything to say about the writing budget for the show but I feel sure they'll agree the $300 we split is not enough considering the ratings and the work involved.

I should think $250 each would be a reasonable boost. If I am in error in not saying $350 please consider my having done so.

. . .

In 1961 I was working in an office adjacent to the main CBS building at 485 Madison Avenue in New York. I received a memo from a CBS vice president. It's hard to believe the same vice president would handle two such disparate matters but he was the same one from whom I got a memo asking that I sign the non-communist oath.

In the memo he said, "I would appreciate very much your not asking to have your building reopened after hours.

"Once the doors are locked for the night—after determining there is no one on the premises—the guards have been instructed not to unlock them except in extreme emergencies."

Dear Mr. Maulsby,

I have your note requesting me not to ask admittance to 46 East 52 Street "after hours." After whose hours?

Garry Moore is leaving New York for thirteen weeks at the end of June and we are trying to get enough shows taped ahead of time to carry us through that period. Writing sixty-five, ten-minute shows entails more work than I am able to accomplish during a vice president's working hours.

I had planned to work both tomorrow, Saturday, and the next day, Sunday. Will I be able to get into this building? If I can't could you make arrangements to cancel *The Garry Moore Show* for thirteen weeks?

May 22, 1962

TO: Lawrence W. Lowman
Personnel Vice President, CBS
FROM: Andrew A. Rooney

Dear Mr. Lowman,

For the past eight months I've been writing the *Calendar* show five days a week with John Mosedale.

The *Calendar* script is usually finished by 7:00 P.M. and has to be retyped, duplicated and delivered to five producers, the director and to Mary Fickett and Harry Reasoner.

It was decided it would be practical to have a male typist who could clean up the script when we finished it, mimeograph it and then deliver it that night to five locations around town.

We had five unsatisfactory candidates and finally settled on a twenty-nine-year-old colored [We were still using "colored" in 1962] man named Ernest Hall. [I've changed his name, although he probably wouldn't care.] He came from Olsen's Employment Agency and was an exceptionally fast typist. A whiz. He didn't look like the all-American boy. His dress was strange but he was pleasant and extremely helpful with everything.

After four months, it was decided he should be put on staff. He filled out the CBS forms and expressed what I thought was an unusual degree of delight over having a steady job. He said he hadn't had anything regular in some time.

Some strange things happened with Ernie around the office. Two television sets disappeared and one day he came to me and asked to borrow $150. He said he had to go see his mother who was sick in Detroit. I doubted his story about his sick mother but loaned him the money and he disappeared for five days. When he returned, his jaw was swollen and his eyes discolored.

A short while later, Tom Wolfe, the *Calendar* producer, told me Ernie had been called the previous evening by the CBS Employment Office and told not to come back to work the next day. They had discovered he had spent a year in a Federal prison in Detroit six years ago.

He was dismissed by CBS, they said, not because of his prison record but because he falsified his CBS application by failing to mention it.

Jack Kiermaier and Tom Wolfe put some pressure on the Employment Office and were told they didn't want to hear any more about it. The case was closed.

They added that Ernie had "been in trouble" in New York as recently as January for breaking into an apartment and that he also had a record as a homosexual.

Ernie came to my office in tears. "Six years ago and I can't lose it," he said. "I was working at a Detroit radio station. They had some contest where people sent in a dollar. One of the executives and I opened a bunch of the envelopes and took a lot of dollars over a period of a month. We got caught and we both went to Federal prison because it was tampering with the U.S. Mail."

"Every time I get a job they find out and I get fired. If I tell them about it first I don't get the job."

"Tell me the truth, Ernie" I asked him. "What about your sick mother in Detroit?"

He said he was homosexual and he was having trouble with his lover. He told me that after they had an argument, his partner had decided to go back to Puerto Rico. Ernie picked up with another man and, unfortunately, his original partner returned unexpectedly to the apartment one night. That accounted for his bruises.

"That's why I needed that $150 to get out of town," he said. "I was scared. Did I thank you?"

He knew it was funny. It's hard to describe how charming Ernie could be. He was quick and disarming, especially about himself.

I asked him about breaking into the apartment. He told a long story about having fallen behind on his rent and the landlady changed the lock on his door. He climbed up the drainpipe on the side of the building to get through a window so he could get his clothes.

He was caught by two cops and charged with "breaking and entering." It didn't matter to the police that it was *his* apartment and *his* own clothes he took.

To make certain Ernie was telling me the truth, I tracked down the court record and called the arresting officer, Patrolman Francis Magan of the Tactical Patrol. He confirmed the story and I have the court record.

I asked Ernie if he had any other problems the Employment office was going to throw at us and he broke down in tears.

"Andy" he said. "I have every problem you can imagine. I'm an ex convict, I'm a drug addict, I'm homosexual . . . and I'm black." [Ernie used "black."]

No one could talk CBS into rehiring Ernie and I knew better than anyone how good he was at his job.

I went to Europe for two weeks and Ernie got two weeks' work typing a novel. I mention this to account for the gap between his dismissal and this note to you.

He said he found it difficult to say but what he said didn't surprise me. He was the youngest of seven children, all boys. His mother wanted a girl desperately and had dressed him as a girl and let his hair grow to his shoulders until he was twelve. He had always had a sex problem he said and had been turned down by Army psychiatrists. I believe the CBS doctor he saw when he started to work here, knew of this.

That's the story. I wish you could find a way to arrange for Ernie to be rehired. Are we—and I'm proud of CBS, I say "we"—are we just talkers about doing the right thing when it comes to being open and forgiving? I believe this man has fine potential for being a happy useful citizen and a good CBS worker. I'm confident enough of Ernie that I'd be willing to post a bond against any loss to CBS caused by him. I have too much to do. I would rather forget this whole thing but this seems important and I hope you can help. If CBS fired all the people who have falsified their employment records or all the people on staff who are homosexual it's going to be very short-handed.

You are the only person who might be able to prevail over the Employment Office. I hope you can help get Ernie Hall reinstated.

Andrew A. Rooney

Short term, the story had an unhappy ending. Ernie was not rehired. Long term, it's a success story. Ernie straightened himself out, got off drugs and has a good job with a big agency as a drug counselor. He travels around the Country making speeches. I've had lunch with him several times in the CBS cafeteria and he's as funny [illegible] his sick mother in Detroit. We laugh about it.

. . .

Jack Kiermaier became head of the CBS News documentary unit in the 1960s. Dick Salant, the president of CBS News, had already approved an idea I had approached him with, to be called "An Essay On Doors."

Jack didn't disapprove but he was understandably unclear about what I intended to do and asked me to explain it.

TO: Jack Kiermaier

"An Essay On Doors" will be taped Saturday, February 29, in Studio No. 3. Harry Reasoner will narrate it. The broadcast is in these four parts:

1. There will be fourteen working doors set up for the cameras in the studio by CBS set designers.

- Hospital door with two small, oval glass windows. They lend drama to a door.
- French doors. We will try to determine why they are called French.
- Swinging saloon doors.
- Victorian brownstone-house double doors, inner and outer.
- Forbidding dentist office door with opaque glass and sign.
- Typical American home front door.
- Closet door.
- Revolving door. (Women never take the first one available.)
- Door on a prison cell
- Two screen doors, one old wooden with a spring that pulls it closed, another modern aluminum one with a pneumatic closer. With scrollwork.
- Swinging dining-room-to-kitchen door.
- Refrigerator door.

Harry will make whatever observations there are in the script about these doors.

2. A still picture piece with about thirty photos of specifically historic, architecturally noteworthy or interesting doors. For instance, we have good pictures of the majestic Ghiberti bronze doors in Florence.

3. A montage of film clips showing the use of doors in dramatic situations, serious and comic. We have some movie clips of Loretta Young sweeping out a French door to the garden.

4. A pantomime study of door manners, mannerisms and problems. Franz Reynders, the pantomimist, will perform in the frame of a suggested door. Opening a door for a woman, getting through one with a bag of groceries etc.

Special effects has about seventeen door sounds they use in certain situations for the soap operas. This will make a brief spot for us.

My intention is to make it apparent that the most ordinary objects around us—doors in this case—hold extraordinary interest when viewed from a good angle or from a sufficient number of different angles. There are a great many things to be said about doors and I'll try to say some of them in the script. There is something basically dramatic about a door because our attitude toward one is markedly different if we are outside, wanting to get in, than it is if we are inside, wanting to get out. I don't have a finished script because it will be easier to fit the words to the pictures than it would be for me to write it first and try to find pictures to fit what I've written.

This isn't very convincing, is it? Find it in your heart to trust me.

"An Essay on Doors" was produced and broadcast.

. . .

Will Rogers, Jr. was elected to Congress before WW II and resigned to enlist in the Army in 1942. I met him in Germany in March 1945. He was commander of a Sherman tank during the rough part of the war and I wrote a story about him for The Stars and Stripes.

Bill and I met again eleven years later when I was hired as "head writer" for the CBS Morning Show. *It was a silly title because there was nothing head about me, but the staff, including Barbara Walters, who did the fashion pieces, was capable and we had a lot of fun.*

Bill never got out from under his famous father's shadow. He was one of the most charming, likeable, bumblingly inept former tank commanders who ever hosted a television show.

CBS had never been able to compete with NBC or ABC in the morning and this may have been the worst of a lot of CBS morning shows. I kept in touch with Bill for years after it ended.

July 7, 1959

Will Rogers, Jr.
Tubac, Arizona

Dear Bill,

What am I doing you ask? You will be hurt to know that *The Morning Show*—"*The Good Morning Show*" was it?—was but the beginning of my retreat from literary respectability. I've sold some magazine things—three, successfully, and this must be a First—to *Readers Digest, Harper's, Look* . . . and *Playboy.*

I'm currently writing a genuinely dreadful show replacing Perry Como on Saturday nights. It is called *Perry Presents* and the other writer is Allen Sherman.

The Perry Como offices are on Park Avenue and Perry has an interesting piece of furniture that turns on its axis. It's an altar where mass can be said on one side and a bar on the other.

Perry seems like a good guy although I haven't seen much of him.

On the first show, we had Hans Conreid as "Our Guest-Host." "Guest-host" meant he was only hired for one night I think. The regular stars were Tony Bennett and Teresa Brewer and, although I wrote for them, we never had much contact.

I don't understand why, when someone intelligent and respectable like Hans Conreid takes a job like that for money, the reviewers say only that it was unfortunate that so talented a fellow was trapped in such a bad show. Why don't they say this about me, a writer? I too am urbane, witty, lovable, fair, intelligent—but what they say about me is not that I was unlucky to have been involved with a bad show. They say, in effect, that the writing is terrible. Was I not as trapped by my need for money as Hans Conreid?

The answer in my mind is that acting is a lot easier than writing and critics never seem to understand that. They almost always say that the acting was fine and the sets by Mielzener de Arutunian were exceptional but they say the writing was lousy. I'm not asking for mercy though. Allen Sherman is very talented and I know how but the writing *is* poor. The critics are right.

I'm writing worse than I know how for money.

It worries me occasionally to think that my taste is superior to my talent.

Please find me when you come to New York, even if it means buying my dinner again. I'd like to ask you to ask me to come out there to your ranch and see a real live horse sometime. I've always wondered whether horses really neigh as much as they always do in the movies.

Well, I guess that's about it for now, Folks. Next week we're going to have Tony Bennett, Gloria De Haven, The Four Lads and a man who has appeared frequently on the Ed Sullivan Show doing interesting tricks with a mah jong set.

Edgar Tafel
Architect

Dear Edgar,

Good luck with your book about Frank Lloyd Wright. I know you are a protégé.

I was working as a writer for one of those CBS morning television shows in about 1956–57 when Will Rogers, Jr. was its reluctant star. We did a lot of interviews and Frank Lloyd Wright agreed to come to our studio one morning. The studio occupied a big section of Grand Central Terminal on the third floor above and parallel to 42nd Street. Three tennis courts now occupy the space we used for a television studio.

Our offices were in the Greybar Building north of Grand Central and connected to it. We walked from there, across the glass catwalks on the third floor at the end of Grand Central, to the studio.

I was commissioned to pick up Frank Lloyd Wright at the Plaza Hotel. I was in awe of him and delighted with the assignment. I was greeted at the door of his suite at the Plaza by a young man and shortly thereafter by Mr. Wright's wife.

They had redone the hotel living room so that it was unrecognizable as a hotel room. It had one huge oriental rug that went up and over everything in the room . . . chairs, sofas, tables, everything.

When he was ready we went down to the waiting limousine. Wright grumbled about everything during the drive from the Plaza to the Vanderbilt Ave. entrance to Grand Central. He detested New York. I love New York—especially Grand Central—but I wasn't going to argue with a grand master of design.

There was access by elevator to our third floor studio but I decided to force a tour on this crusty old genius. I took him down the marble steps off Vanderbilt and walked him kitty-corner, past the clock in the center of the waiting room, to the elevators in a little hall on the north side toward Lexington Avenue. This bank of elevators went when they tore down the Terminal Building to put up the Pan Am Building.

I recall clearly that when we got to the elevators toward the Lexington Avenue side, Wright stopped and looked back across the busy room. Five thousand people were going in every direction. The sun's rays were slanting down toward the information booth from the windows above where the Kodak picture is now.

"It is a grand building, isn't it?" he said, almost apologetically and I accepted it as a retraction for all the terrible things he'd been saying about everything else in the City.

We went to the third floor on the elevator and started across the catwalk. You've done that, haven't you? It's one of the great sights in New York City. Thousands of purposeful people going their own directions and with doors and stairs and levels enough for all of them crisscrossing Grand Central Terminal.

Midway across the catwalk, Wright stopped and neither of us said anything. He must have stood there for more than five minutes and I didn't speak because I knew nothing I had to say could match what he was thinking. I finally had to tell him we were due very shortly in the studio and he reluctantly finished his crossing of the catwalk.

The whole incident gave me a great feeling because I thought I'd had some affect on Frank Lloyd Wright's opinion of my city and I knew he could never think completely negatively about it again after his visit to Grand Central.

Another time a year later, we were doing a story about the opening of Wright's Guggenheim Museum on Fifth Avenue. I was talking to the engineer in charge of construction about its unique, spiral design. The engineer told me that after he looked at the plans for the first time, he talked to Wright. He told me he had said, "But Mr. Wright. We don't have material that will do what you have drawn."

The engineer said Wright looked at him and said, "That's not my problem."

These are my Frank Lloyd Wright stories. Use them as you wish.

. . .

The Writers' Guild has a pay scale that depends on the length of a broadcast. In 1965 Don Hewitt produced a show about Frank Sinatra which I wrote. There was a question about how much I should be paid.

Memo To: Bob McCarthy, Business Affairs

I have your request for information about how much of the one hour Frank Sinatra documentary I wrote.

In looking for some guideline to satisfy your request I timed the song Sinatra sang in the show called "September of My Years." From beginning to end it ran 4:20 but with a stopwatch, I determined that words were actually coming out of Sinatra's mouth for only 1:35. Before I say how much of the show I wrote, could you please tell me how much of that song Sinatra sang?

While I did not write sixty minutes of narration, if Frank gets paid for singing the whole song, I should be paid for writing the whole show.

The following letter to my friend and boss, Bill Leonard, at the time a vice president of CBS News, is one I would probably not write today. It makes statements that are no longer true about television news although I'm pleased at my anticipation of the magazine shows like 60 Minutes.

February 3, 1967

Bill Leonard
Vice President
CBS News

Bill,

This is by way of accepting your invitation to comment on the four hour and ten half-hour television broadcasts CBS News has sold to the insurance company.

Everyone has become so accustomed to television news being good, honest and reliable that they forget what it would be like if we pursued circulation like the magazines or the bad papers. None of us wants to lower our standards. We do have another obligation though and that is to attract large numbers of people to watch good things.

There are some honest tricks to be used to attract a crowd. We already use some of them, tentatively. For instance, while news doesn't like to admit it, the star system is in effect on many of its broadcasts. People like what they get familiar with so, just as newspapers use bylines, television repeatedly uses familiar reporters. I think as many people tune in to see Walter Cronkite or Chet Huntley and David Brinkley as tune in to see the news.

British journalism, bad as it is, sells great numbers of newspapers with its tacky style of first-person journalism. ("I have just seen the body of Adolf Hitler's lover.")

The star system creates its own monster because it's hard for someone to be a star without acting like one but when you decide what to call the series, it should include Harry Reasoner's name.

The series looks like an opportunity for the news division to get into the network schedule with more time. We ought to be able to compete for the audience against situation comedies if our broadcasts are good enough.

The pieces in the shows should have a style of their own and a logo of their own. They could be one subject per hour or as many as three or four shorter ones. It might be worth spending $7,500 to get an animated opening to be used at the top on all of them. The Tuesday night documentary hour this year had nothing familiar about it. There was nothing to remind viewers that it was a series. We had some good broadcasts but they suffered from lack of identification. They didn't have a name they could call their own. There was no identifying musical theme so they didn't even have a familiar sound.

I say these things now because you asked me and because if my hour documentary "Barry Goldwater's Arizona" is to be part of the series, it should conform to the style of the others.

You ask me for ideas but ideas are a dime a dozen. It's getting good producers who can do anything with an idea that are hard to find. How something is done makes more difference than the idea or subject matter.

Here are some things I would like to do:

- The ten best-known streets in the world. It would be fun to arbitrarily choose ten and put together an hour. For some, I'd rent a room with a view of the street and install a photographer in the window to film hours of anything going on below. You'd hope to get lucky but even if you weren't, it could be interesting. (There are twenty-three women's shoe stores on Fifth Avenue between 34th and 59th.)

- Document the battle for space between things and people. Our population is headed for 200 million next year. We cut off three feet of the sidewalk on each side of 46th Street to make room for more cars and plant a tree in the middle of what's left of the sidewalk to make it attractive to more pedestrians—for whom there is no space left. Then we have to hold the tree up with guy wires.
- A Profile of the Pentagon as a building. People are familiar with it in a general way but don't know it's the biggest (and most confusing) building in the world with rings of corridors within rings of corridors. It takes anyone working there months to find his way around—and then he's transferred.
- Famous People At Ease. Maybe this is too light but it would be interesting fun to film a dozen or so politicians, entertainers, sports figures on vacation. Chevalier on the Queen Mary, Dean Rusk in the Canary Islands, J. Paul Getty on the Onassis yacht. Maybe we could get Manchester and Jackie water-skiing double at the Cape. I hear they did it.
- For three years Harry Reasoner has wanted to take off in a car with a camera crew and send back a piece nightly for the Cronkite news. Obviously it is never going to happen but the odyssey idea could be made into a good hour. He would talk to people, find out how many customers the gas station owner outside Great Falls, Idaho, has on an average day and how much he makes on a quart of oil. It would comprise Americana details of small events and people.
- Restaurants in the U.S. or eating out in America. What's good and bad about our food and the establishments that sell it. It would be fun to film some of the restaurants I avoid. For examples, I avoid:

1. A place that calls itself Polynesian in Miami and has flaming torches outside.
2. Any place that advertises itself as having "HOME COOKING." If I want home cooking, I'll eat home.
3. A restaurant with a sign in the window that says "OPEN."
4. A restaurant with a sign in the window saying "HELP WANTED."
5. I never eat where I sleep. No matter how far I have to drive, I don't eat in the hotel I'm staying in.
6. Any restaurant on top of the tallest building in town—particularly if it turns.

The hour should do something serious about food, too.

Whether I'm involved in this series or not I hope they are attacked with some special enthusiasm. A good, regular magazine-style show could be a big thing for television news and I'd like to be part of it.

Or isn't all that the kind of comment you were asking for?

. . .

Eric Barnouw

Dear Mr. Barnouw,

A friend sent me page 134 of your book *The Sponsor*. Even good friends find it difficult not to take pleasure in nasty comments about a writer's work.

Of the six documentaries you chose to illustrate your contention that topics for documentaries on network television broadcasts were chosen to attract sponsors' money, five were mine. I wish I could find a more effective way to say it but, simply put, you are wrong. More strongly put, you don't know what you're talking about.

The documentaries "A Birdseye View Of Scotland," "An Essay On Women," "Mr. Rooney Goes To Dinner" were my ideas. The question of sponsorship did not enter my mind. I could not tell you now whether they were sponsored or not. It is of no interest to me whatsoever. I leave six one minute holes in an hour and, as a writer, would admit to welcoming the pauses just as a writer of books welcomes the chance to end a chapter so he can start fresh with another thought without having to make some tenuous transition. This is my only interest in commercials.

I'll say it again. You are wrong. Can you possibly believe that? Can you believe that a broadcast of mine often goes on the air without my knowledge of whose commercials will be inserted into it, if any?

I also hope you believe we do not show anything to any agency or company representative in advance to attract them to sponsorship or to show them what their commercials will be surrounded by because that is the fact.

. . .

Reed Irvine
Accuracy in Media
Washington, D.C.

Dear Mr. Irvine,

Your letter to William S. Paley regarding the broadcast "FDR: The Man Who Changed America," read by Henry Fonda, has been forwarded to me because I wrote the script, including the portion that offends you. Your letter offends me.

I would like to say first that if you are looking for a conspiracy, you are looking in the wrong place. The writing was mine alone and except for research material, I did not take advice from anyone. Nor was any pressed on me. The management of CBS News trusts my judgment even if, as is inevitable, it occasionally fails them.

I am fifty-five years old and grew up in Albany so I know something of Roosevelt but memories and opinions formed half from fact and half from legend, don't meet CBS's standards so it was necessary for me to start from the beginning and learn about Roosevelt.

My father made $8,000 all through The Depression so I was one of the rich kids. Dad hated Roosevelt as many did. Years later, we were driving with a friend and came to a toll booth. When the attendant handed her back a Roosevelt dime in change, she threw it to the road in disgust.

I read six books, looked through dozens more and was provided with excerpts from others by two competent researchers Richard Tuckerman and Jane Bradford. Mr. Tuckerman, a CBS staff researcher, is a retired USAF colonel.

You may be interested to know—and may draw negative inferences from it—that I was surprised by one thing in all my reading. It was that Roosevelt, rather than destroying the free enterprise system as he has been accused of doing, saved it. I had never realized the extent of the communist movement in the United States. I am not talking so much about Soviet infiltration, which obviously existed, but the more serious feeling on the part of many Americans, that our system simply wasn't working.

To summarize the life and times of Franklin Roosevelt in fifty minutes is not an easy job and the kind of writing that goes into a script tailored to fit pictures is a form of shorthand. The writer has nine or seven or fourteen seconds to say it.

The facts are that in the action against the homeless tent city people in Washington, two veterans were killed, two infants were killed. In writing the script, I did not distinguish between the police under the direction of General Padget Glassford, acting on orders from The White House, and the troops under General MacArthur.

I do know that the veterans were killed by the police and the infants were killed by the troops after MacArthur moved across the Anacosta. It did not and does not seem important to me.

Do you really feel that putting those two things together "distorts" the truth of the whole situation? Do you think it is really inaccurate to say that his order to attack the veterans hurt Hoover? It does not matter that you think he did the right thing or that I think he did the wrong thing. The fact is, most Americans at the time felt he did the wrong thing. That is not an opinion. It is a fact.

You apparently do not believe that any inaccuracies or bias that emanate from here are a matter of execution, not design or intent.

I have never met William Paley but next time you write a letter of complaint to him about something I have written, I'd be pleased to have you call it to his attention by mentioning my name. It might give me more stature here.

. . .

Perry Wolff
CBS

Dear Skee,

There's something I want to tell you before you hear it from the other kids on the street.

I've filed a mild complaint with Mr. Leonard in regard to the reorganization of the documentary division at CBS News. I've said that I like you as a friend and admire you as a producer but don't want you as a boss.

I can't imagine why in the world the idea of being my boss would appeal to you, either.

The fact is, I don't want anybody as a boss. Realizing this is impractical, I'd like to have a boss who doesn't come as close to working the same side of the street as you do. You represent the whole trouble with television. A guy comes along with talent as a writer and capability as a producer and first thing you know he realizes those two functions are harder than being a boss so he becomes an executive producer and starts feeding off the less talented work of others like myself.

It should be reassuring to you to know that I don't have money enough to quit over this issue.

. . .

In 1970, Harry Reasoner left CBS to go to ABC. I got into an argument at CBS over a documentary I'd done called "An Essay On War" which they didn't want to broadcast as I'd done it and ended up quitting over it. Everyone ought to quit a job once or twice in a lifetime.

CBS sold me "An Essay On War" for what it had cost to make and PBS bought it for a price that gave me a good profit. It was then syndicated by the Encyclopedia Brittanica Films and sold to hundreds of schools. It was a get-well financial experience.

For the first year after I left CBS, I worked at a good and creative show on public television called The Great American Dream Machine, produced by Al Perlmutter and Jack Willis. After a satisfying year there, Harry asked me to come to ABC to write and produce a series of hour-long documentaries for him. I did that.

After eight months, Dick Salant, the president of CBS News, asked me to come back. I did that, too. Elmer Lower was president of ABC News:

Dear Elmer,

You and Bill Sheehan and a variety of attractive reasons for staying at ABC made it difficult for me to decide to leave. I don't know as I could spell out why I'm doing it. I've enjoyed being here and enjoyed the capable people I've come to know.

Harry is as good a friend as I have and that won't change, but we both understand that while we've made out well together, neither of us is dependent on the other.

As I see your new show, *The Reasoner Report* developing, it does not appear to be the sort of thing I could be most help on. I have always wanted to work on a nonfiction smorgasbord or a news variety show aimed at attracting large numbers of people. One of the networks will do it at some point but it's not what *The Reasoner Report* will be.

My old friend, the impossible Ernie Leiser, is a capable producer with great experience at the executive level. You were smart to take him away from CBS. He certainly strengthens your department. It has always been my feeling though that the on-camera person ought to be dominant on any broadcast. It is difficult to write and produce for someone when there is a layer of authority between me and the star of the show.

Harry is not always interested in taking as much authority as I like to push on him and because Ernie is such a strong personality I know I would end up trying to please him first and Harry second. It wouldn't be good for the broadcast.

And then, as much as I've enjoyed it here, I think my heart belongs to CBS. It doesn't have to make sense.

CBS Business Affairs,

Am I being asked to sign a form saying I do not plan to give to the United Way as a CBS employee?

I don't sign forms for insurance salesman saying I don't want to buy their policy. If I had to sign a form attesting to my disinterest in giving to every charity seeking money from me, it would be a full time job.

This form seems like a crude pressure tactic and I am curious about what benefit it is to CBS in being a major contributor to the United Way.

In our hometown, I don't tell the United Way that "I gave at the office" and I am under no obligation to tell anyone at the office that "I gave at home"—although we do, of course.

. . .

John Fischer
Chicago, Illinois

I'm responding to your request for information about Arthur Godfrey for the history of television you're writing because I am so often annoyed when he is omitted.

If someone wrote a history of the United States and did not mention George Washington, critics might reasonably complain that the book was incomplete.

Godfrey wasn't my best friend but I wrote for him for five years and no legitimate history of television could be done without including him as a major part of it.

Recently CBS broadcast a history of its first fifty years without ever mentioning its single, all time, most popular star, Arthur Godfrey. I fail to understand how that happened. Godfrey was not only the biggest star CBS television ever had, he was the biggest money-producing entertainer CBS has ever had. Bigger than Jack Benny because he did more. His two nighttime shows, *Talent Scouts* and *Arthur Godfrey and His Friends* and his hour and a half daily morning show occupied more time on the air than any other personality ever has. He dominated nighttime and daytime ratings like no one else ever has and it's a mystery to me how the producer of CBS's own history of its first fifty years could fail to mention Godfrey's name once.

CBS executives never liked Godfrey because of his independence. He did what he felt like doing. It is probably for this reason that CBS has contributed to burying his memory with him. CBS bought a theater on Broadway at 53rd Street in about 1950 and turned it into the studio from which Godfrey's two nighttime shows emanated. Ed Sullivan's show, called *Toast Of The Town*, was done at the same theater. Sullivan's ratings were consistently lower than Godfrey's but after both men were gone, they named it The Ed Sullivan Theater. It's as if someone who didn't know any better called the Washington Monument the Lincoln Tower.

For reasons I don't understand, some people make the history books and others don't. It has no direct relation to accomplishment. Fame has a life of its own. Some people become legends, known long after they've departed. Others, equally famous in life, are all but forgotten shortly after they die. Godfrey is destined to be one of those. He'd hate it.

Ed Sullivan made his reputation as a gossip columnist with *The Daily News*. He was a pointer on television. He pointed to the next act and gave their names. It was the performers, not Sullivan, who made the show popular.

Godfrey, on the other hand, did his own show. *Arthur Godfrey and His Friends* was 90 percent Godfrey and 10 percent "Friends." On his *Talent Scouts* show, he was instrumental in bringing to public attention such previously unknown people as Steve Lawrence, Tony Bennett, Pat

Boone, the Smothers Brothers, Leslie Uggams, Vic Damone, Beverly Sills, Wally Cox and the McGuire Sisters.

Godfrey not only did his two top-rated evening television shows but he outrated the soap operas for an hour and a half every weekday morning. In his first year on television, not long after CBS President Frank Stanton brought him from Washington where he was on radio, Godfrey's morning show was broadcast simultaneously on radio and television. In his second year, he brought in six million dollars to a company struggling to survive. And he doesn't get mentioned in a show purporting to be a history of CBS's first fifty years?

In the 1951–52 season Godfrey's *Talent Scouts* show was No. 1, Ed Wynn and the *Texaco Star Theater* was No. 2, *I Love Lucy* No. 3, Red Skelton No. 4 and *Arthur Godfrey and His Friends*, No. 6.

The following year *I Love Lucy* was No. 1 and Godfrey's shows were Nos. 2 and 3.

Ed Sullivan was not in the top twenty-five.

Again in 1953–54, *Talent Scouts* was No. 3, *Arthur Godfrey and His Friends* No. 6. Sullivan's *Toast Of The Town* was nowhere in sight.

To give you some idea of Godfrey's competition that year, Groucho Marx's show, *You Bet Your Life*, was No. 4, *The Bob Hope Show* No. 5. *The Jack Benny Show* was No. 16.

The only area in which Ed Sullivan exceeded Godfrey was in longevity. Ed Sullivan's *Toast Of The Town* ran for twenty-three years. *Talent Scouts* was on for eleven years, *Arthur Godfrey and His Friends* for ten.

Godfrey was not the only missing person on the fifty-year show. Although Carol Burnett was featured, Carol Burnett made her reputation appearing on *The Garry Moore Show*. They couldn't find time to mention the great Garry Moore, either.

The producers should have been taking, not giving, a history lesson.

Good luck with your work on the history of television. Use what you wish of this.

. . .

December, 1983

Memo to Don Hewitt
60 Minutes, Producer

While I'm not comfortable having to ask, I am asking you to reconsider the way I am introduced at the top of the broadcast. ". . . and more" doesn't seem like enough as a way of noting that I'll be on. My name should be mentioned although I have no interest in mentioning it myself, as the others do.

Let me know what you decide. I haven't quit in years.

. . .

Most of us who were colleagues of Eric Sevareid's didn't think of ourselves as equals and were never easy in his presence. I had tentatively used his name in a piece I did for 60 Minutes.

March 4, 1988

Eric Sevareid,
Washington, D.C.

Dear Eric,

I was mighty pleased and relieved to get your note. I had thought of calling to ask permission to use your name in that manner but decided against it for fear you'd say no.

Your essay on corporate insultability last night was delightful and your reference to the American Bar Association reminds me of two stories.

Right after the war I'd written a book that MGM bought. I was in the producer's office one day—a tyrant named Voldemar Vetluguin—going over what I thought was a screenplay, when his assistant entered in an agitated state, waving a formal-looking letter.

The American Bar Association had written to report that it had conducted a study and their figures showed that in the last seventy-three MGM movies in which actors portrayed lawyers, they had been shown as dishonest or in an otherwise unfavorable light sixty-nine times. The ABA demanded to know what MGM was going to do about it.

Vetluguin paused briefly then looked at his assistant and said "Sixty-nine out of seventy-three? Write back and tell them we gave lawyers a break."

The other was a Marx Brothers legal story. During the same period, the Marx Brothers set out to make the movie they were calling *A Night in Casablanca*. Warner Brothers lawyers set out to get an injunction to inhibit the Marx Brothers from using the name "Casablanca" in their title because of the Warner movie the year before by that name with Humphrey Bogart and Lauren Bacall.

Groucho wrote the *Hollywood Reporter* and said he was taking legal action, too. He was enjoining Warner Brothers from using the word "Brothers" in their company title because the Marx were brothers before the Warners were born.

Warners wisely dropped their legal initiative.

It meant a great deal to me to get your note. I don't want to make you nervous but you're a hero of mine.

Warm regards to you and to the talented, not to mention beautiful, Suzanne.

John Sharnik was a vice president at CBS News in charge of the documentary unit. Another friend, Skee Wolff was my executive producer and both understood I thought that was too many layers of authority. When we were about to screen the broadcast, John wrote me a note to make sure I invited the executive producer to see it.

John,

You underestimate my skill dealing with an executive producer. Of course I invited Skee because I knew you'd want it.

It is part of my knowing how to deal with a vice president.

Anyway, it's better for me that way. When the executive producer and the vice president attend the same screening and each has ideas about what's wrong and how it has to be changed, they usually disagree more with each other than with the producer. What happens then is that it doesn't double the number of changes I have to make, it halves them.

Andy

. . .

Van Gordon Sauter was president of CBS Sports and then president of CBS News.

Van,

I have received a copy of your memo titled "Revised Sports Standards Manual" in which you emphasize the importance of honesty and integrity.

If you're going to introduce honesty and integrity into television sports coverage, you're going to take all the fun out of it. You're the kind of guy who probably wants honest professional wrestling.

John Oswald
CBS Management

Dear Mr. Oswald,

You are being unnecessarily sensitive about a small joke. I don't think my suggestion on *60 Minutes* that the cleaning people ate our cookies carries with it any implication that they're dishonest. We have a good relationship with the people who clean these offices every night and their reputation for honesty is impeccable.

I leave cameras, tape recorders and even cash on my desk sometimes when I leave at night and in the seven years we've been in these offices, not a single item has been missing.

I do not consider a few missing cookies from an open box to be theft of any kind. They were obviously there so anyone could help themselves.

. . .

Russ Bensley was the only television news producer I ever saw who could sit in a dark screening room with a typewriter, watch twenty minutes of raw footage and then hand an editor a couple of sheets of paper with cuts that took the film down to a minute and twelve seconds.

Russ and his wife, Pat, a popular television director, left the business in the 1970s to run a horse farm.

March 3, 1990

Dear Pat and Russ,

Your farm sounds the right size and I might drop in as you suggest. I've never understood why you handle horse manure with a pitchfork and your farm sounds like the right place for me to find out. It's the kind of information that might come in handy in television.

It's going to be hard to drop in though because I'm not sure where the "MI" in your address is.

Of all the postal abbreviations, MI is the worst. I don't know what state MI represents. If you're near the South Bend airport it makes sense that you live in Indiana but MI certainly wouldn't stand for Indiana. You wouldn't live in MIssissippi and MIssouri is out of the question because you'd be raising mules not horses. MInnesota is possible but that would be quite a drive from South Bend. Maine is ME, so that's out. By the process of elimination, I conclude that your farm must be in MIchigan.

Everyone still misses both of you. I'll amend that. *Almost* everyone still misses you. You were too definite about what you knew should be done not to have left a few people behind who are glad you're on a horse farm giving horses, rather than them, a hard time.

You wouldn't know the place and take that as good for you. There's been a marked decline in everything since you left—which seemed like a low point to you.

I don't want to lie to you. I'm writing on a computer now and this is a form letter.

Warm regards,

· · ·

For almost ten years I wrote documentaries and 60 Minutes *reports for Harry Reasoner. He was one of the best writers in television news but he was indifferent to the work.*

He enjoyed all the good things that being a successful television correspondent brought him but he never went to work with the same enthusiasm that Mike Wallace did, for example.

I realized, after writing the words a lot of different people read on camera over the years, that it was easier to write for someone like Harry, who could have done it as well or better without me, than it was writing for someone who didn't write well at all.

Harry died in 1991, suffering from several maladies and under circumstances that were not clear. His family was never satisfied with exactly what killed him and looked everywhere for answers.

Ellen Reasoner
Westport, Connecticut

Dear Ellen,

Your father and I were close friends even when we weren't getting along—which was often. He was so brilliant and such an idiot. He was maddening and lovable.

You will be making a mistake if you let the mystery surrounding his death consume you. Whatever the immediate cause of his demise, he died because of the kind of person he was. The kind of person your father and my dear friend was, led him to smoke too much, to drink too much and to make several foolish friendships.

Love his memory as I do but move on.

Leslie Moonves
President
CBS Entertainment
Hollywood, California

Dear Les,

There must be fifty new stage plays that open on (or off) Broadway every year. Most are not hits. They're good and bad but most of them have something.

It has frequently occurred to me that a group of competent writers could search through a thousand of the current plays and plays from years past and find fifty or a hundred that could be turned into a television series called *Broadway*.

I got no acknowledgment.

. . .

Television executives get hundreds of unsolicited ideas a year and don't dare acknowledge them because of the constant threat of lawsuits.

Shellie Gerould
Gillett, Pennsylvania

Dear Shellie,

I couldn't think why I'd saved your letter in a heap of good letters until I got to the bottom of it. I was caught by your comment about Dan Rather and what you feel is the pejorative nature of many of his references to President Bush.

Conservatives have always complained about the liberal slant of television journalism and, even though I'm one of the liberals and concur with the angle of the slant, I too object to any kind of editorial intrusion on the news.

. . .

Suzanne St. Pierre was a producer at 60 Minutes *who married Eric Sevareid in 1979. When Eric fell ill, someone accused him of being a hypochondriac. Without hesitating, Eric said "Hypochondriacs get sick too, you know." Eric was very sick and he died in 1992.*

Dear Suzanne,

Because of those few years we spent as office neighbors, I have good and warm memories of you. You've come to my mind a dozen times a day since Eric died. I know what a hard time you had toward the end and it must never have been easy being in love with a legend. Great men are never easy and Eric was great.

I called Bill Leonard in Mougin the day Eric died and as we talked, two grown men wept long distance. It had not occurred to me that Eric's death would bring tears to my eyes.

. . .

Peggy Noonan, a bright, attractive, talented, Catholic girl wrote radio essays for Dan Rather for several years and then wrote speeches for Ronald Reagan and George Bush from an office adjacent to The White House. I mention her attributes because they seemed like an unlikely combination to anyone who knew her. I knew her.

Dear Peggy,

It was good to hear from you. I was going to write and tell you I met your brother at a urinal at the track in Saratoga. He was fine.

Apology only has one g. I guess you've never done much of it. And I know damn well your boss never has. The word wouldn't come up much in the speeches you write for him.

I hope the man you are engaged to marry is a left wing atheist. You need some balance in your life.

CBS has not been as good a place to be as it was when you were here. Everyone feels fired—even those who weren't. They got rid of some dead wood but a company, like a forest, needs some dead wood. They got rid of a lot of wood here that wasn't dead, too. A great many of us are feeling we are loyal to something that no longer exists.

I've been at CBS through seven company presidents. I trust you understand that this is unlikely to happen to you in your present job.

. . .

After I'd done a piece for 60 Minutes *in which I indicated, as a little joke without actually saying so, that I preferred Maker's Mark bourbon, Don Hewitt, the* 60 Minutes *producer, got a call from a columnist accusing me of accepting a case of bourbon as a payoff for the plug.*

It turned out to be a satisfying little episode for me when Don called and asked, in a frantic voice,

"Did they send you a case of bourbon?" Don asked.

Yes I said.

"Andy, you gotta send it back," Don said.

I told him he was a week late. It was delivered the Monday following the show but I know the rules and had returned it to the sender the same day with this note.

Bruce Levine
Astoria, New York

Dear Mr. Levine,

Thank you for the case of Maker's Mark. It hurts me more than it hurts you that I have to return it. I was pleased you sent it—it completes the joke—but it would be wrong of me to accept it.

Maybe sometime in the future we'll meet under circumstances in which you can buy me a drink. I don't think one would compromise my integrity.

Several weeks ago I met Bill Samuels, Maker's Mark president, and I was encouraged that he assured me there is no danger of their liquor deteriorating in quality in view of its increasing sales. He explained that he can always get the same good grain but good water was becoming a problem. He said they draw from several wells on their property that have limited capacity so they recently had city water piped in. This enables them to conserve their well water for exclusive use in the bourbon without using any of it for other purposes.

While I prefer Maker's Mark, I enjoy Wild Turkey, Old Grand Dad, Old Forester and one or two others. Jim Beam is unacceptable and I admire the Jack Daniels organization for being able to sell a mediocre whiskey, that is not a true bourbon, so well. I haven't been much taken with the single barrel bourbons. For one thing, I don't like anything higher than ninety proof.

Thanks again.

Arnold A. Rivin
Santa Fe, New Mexico

Dear Mr. Rivin,

Thank you for calling CBS's attention to the imposter doing commercials in what he thinks is an Andy Rooney style. There are a lot of them around the country and it's irritating but it's probably more trouble than it's worth to try to stop them. I'm not clear about what the law is and don't have enough interest to try to find out.

Several years ago Meineke Muffler was using someone to look and sound like me and we did the enclosed piece for 60 *Minutes*. Our hidden camera caught one Meineke franchise selling us a muffler we didn't need. They took their commercial off the air.

This is a transcript of the piece as aired.

For most of my years in television, I was a writer. Someone else stood in front of the camera and read what I wrote.

The arrangement was fine with me but then, for some reason that escapes me now, I started reading my own things on camera.

It seems wrong that I get paid more now for reading them than I did then for writing them. And there are drawbacks.

One of the drawbacks is the number of people who do imitations of me. Some of them are good and make me laugh . . . some of them are embarrassingly bad and make me mad.

RICH LITTLE (AS ANDY ROONEY): Have you ever noticed how some people can't come out and say "Thrifty price for everyone." Have you ever noticed that?

Joe Piscopo (as Andy Rooney): Well, do you ever notice people watch a lot of TV. I just don't understand it . . . unless they're watching me.

Orange Buick Salesman (as Andy Rooney): Have you ever wondered why most car dealerships use this little asterisk symbol in their ads?

Rooney: The worst of the imitations are the ones using my voice to sell something like second-hand cars.

One bad imitation has been used as a sales pitch for Meineke Mufflers on radio.

Voice (as Rooney): Ever watch TV commercials? I do. My favorites are the ones that show this poor Meineke Muffler guy. He's besieged by every nut in the world screaming "I'm not going to pay a lot for this muffler."

Rooney: I own a 1977 Ford Station Wagon that started sounding loud awhile ago so I decided to go to Meineke and see what kind of a deal I could get.

First I had the muffler checked someplace else.

Rooney: Does it need a new muffler?

Mechanic: No. The pipe . . . they just came disconnected. It's got to be reconnected.

Rooney: So there's really not much to be done, is there?

Mechanic: No.

Rooney: Then I took the car to a Meineke shop.

Meineke Worker: All you need . . .

Rooney: What's that?

Meineke Worker: All you need is a muffler and a couple of clamps. About $40 bucks . . . $45 with the clamps. All right, should I do it? $45 plus tax.

Rooney: Yeh. Right.

VOICE (AS ROONEY): I really didn't pay a lot for my muffler. I wonder why?

ROONEY: I didn't pay a lot for this muffler. The question is: Did I need a new muffler at all?

Every once in a while someone hears one of these commercials and asks if it's really me. I don't answer. If anyone's dumb enough to believe I'd endorse a product for money, I don't care what they think.

And then, sometimes people suggest that I ought to sue. Well, I'm NOT going to sue a lot for this muffler.

. . .

Richard Perkins
Palos Verdes Estates, California

Dear Mr Perkins,

Hughes Rudd was a great friend. I went to his funeral last year in Washington. There were a lot of good people and good friends of Hughes's there. It's funny that he had so many friends because he was hard to be good friends with. He kept getting drunk and telling you to go to hell.

Among other unlikely friends, Sally Quinn was there with her husband, Ben Bradlee. Sally and Hughes had done the *CBS News Morning Show* together.

We were all surprised that he was buried in Arlington. Hughes never talked about it but he was a decorated Piper Cub artillery spotter with two Purple Hearts acquired when he was hit by Wehrmacht rifle fire from the ground.

Mr. Bill Moyers
Public Affairs Television

Dear Bill,

We spent a week with Cronkite sailing in the Virgin Islands and, while I enjoy being with Walter and Betsy, I'm lukewarm on everything else about sailing.

To fill in the long hours between getting up and and going to bed, I took along your book, *The Power of Myth*, and actually read it. It's the first book I've really read since *Lorna Doone*.

I was taken by Joseph Campbell's charm, knowledge and intellect and impressed with the job you did of bringing him out without intruding. You also revealed more about yourself than I'd previously known.

I filled the margins with notes and I was going to extract my observations and send them to you and then it occurred to me that you must be swamped by people who wish to agree or disagree with something in the book and I've decided to spare you. The single idea of Campbell's that I disagree with most is the statement "Reason puts you in touch with God."

Reason leads you up a dead end street if you're looking for God.

. . .

When Charles Kuralt died I spoke at the memorial service held for him in New York. His brother wrote to thank me.

Dear Wallace,

Your letter was a treat to read.

It's still very sad. Charles was an enigma and I wouldn't be surprised to hear that even you found him enigmatic at times. We will all remember with great affection though, how good he was to be with and I hope the world does not soon forget his towering talent. He did it all so effortlessly that it looked easy but if it was easy, how come no one else in the history of television has ever done it so well?

. . .

This was written to a television time salesman in Los Angeles who complained bitterly about something negative I'd written about television news.

Dear Jim, (His name was actually Fred but I'm respecting his request for anonymity.)

Biting the hand that feeds me, you say?

I can't deny I make my living from television news but does that mean I don't have the right to be critical of it? You don't have to leave the United States because you're critical of its government sometimes. You don't leave home because you get mad at your wife or kids. You try to improve things.

You ask what I'd do to improve the evening news broadcasts at the networks as if you thought I couldn't come up with any ideas. I do have some suggestions and I wouldn't give them to you if I didn't think they were practical and would work without bankrupting the company.

It's my opinion that the number of people watching network television news is substantially less than it was five or ten years ago because there is less news on those shows. A half-hour news show has about twenty-one minutes of editorial content, with fewer words than are on just two pages of a newspaper with pictures. A news broadcast is not so worthwhile a way to spend a half hour as it once was. People don't sit down and say that to themselves, it's just a sense they have.

To begin with, I would startle the affiliates by announcing that, whether they liked it or not, the evening news broadcast would, henceforth, be one hour long. If all the magazine shows are so successful, I fail to understand why a good, hard news hour would not attract a substantial audience.

I would repeat the hour, as broadcast, from 8 A.M. TO 9 A.M. every morning.

News on television is thin because they do not have staff enough to do it right. I'd hire more good, young news people and hire back some of the good old ones who got fired to save money.

I'd talk to the anchormen and women and magazine correspondents making $8 million a year and I'd say to them "Look, let's spread this money a little thinner so the people who are not anchormen, make more and you make less." They're all good guys. They'd do it. It's just that none of them wants to be first.

I'd reopen all the network news bureaus that have been closed over the years. I'd pay correspondents to be in places we wouldn't need them very often, just in case something happened there. There are stories everywhere but someone has to be there to tell them.

I'd eliminate any commercial that was offensive or otherwise in bad taste. Because I believe it discourages people from watching the news, I'd eliminate commercials for false teeth glue, incontinence pants, laxatives, hemorrhoid cures and medicine for diarrhea.

When people are sitting in their living room at the end of the day watching the news, reading the newspaper, relaxing and talking about their day , they do not want this pleasant hour ruined by intrusive commercials that they can't pretend they aren't hearing.

We would not run commercials for the magic potion for male sex, Viagra. Bob Dole could go get himself a real job.

I would forbid what are called "promos." A news broadcast would not be allowed to advertise itself or claim as "exclusive" a story everyone else has.

The broadcast would not be allowed to try to attract viewers for tomorrow night's program by teasing them with a snippet they can see if they tune in "tomorrow." It isn't news if they have the story today and don't tell everyone what it is until tomorrow. That's history.

We'd reduce the number of feature stories and feature sections with their own names currently replacing real news.

We would fire any individual or polling organization involved in trying to determine what news the public wants to hear. The decision about what news the public gets would be left solely to the judgment of news editors. The decision about whether a story is broadcast would be based on whether it is something the public ought to know, not on whether it's something the public wants to hear.

Medical stories suggesting an imminent cure for cancer, heart disease, lyme disease, arthritis, headcolds, diabetes and Alzheimer's would not be broadcast until the cure is a fact, not a wish.

If we produced the best television news broadcast there ever was night after night, I'm convinced it would attract an audience and pay for itself.

When this happens maybe you'll want to move to New York and sell commercials for classy products on the revised news broadcasts.

PART THREE

The Viewers Write

Most of the suggestions I get for pieces to do on 60 Minutes, *are things I've already done. People are always sending me fat envelopes of junk mail they've received and suggest I do something about junk mail. I've done junk mail.*

I am not really open to suggestions but every once in a while I get a good one.

Craig Fox
Newbury Park, California

Dear Craig,

Thanks for the suggestion about horns. I remember when horns went A OO GAH.

I'll try to find out whether a Cadillac has a more expensive-sounding horn than a Ford.

For your trouble, I'll let you know before it goes on.

. . .

Adam Dolgins
New York, New York

Dear Mr. Dolgins,

Don Hewitt sent me your letter and the copy of *Rock Names*, referring to rock musicians.

I looked through the book and was very impressed with all the work you did and monumentally disinterested in the information you gathered. You might find a small market for the book. I hope so because good reporting should be rewarded, no matter what the subject.

As someone who tries to appeal to a broad audience in both my television work and my newspaper column, I often worry about the great number of people who are attracted to something I don't know or care anything about. Part of it is age, of course, but there's something else going on there, too. I never understood the appeal of Frank Sinatra when I was sixteen or Elvis when I was fifty. Now I like Sinatra but feel I will never like rock.

. . .

Jacqueline Armstrong

Dear Jacqueline,

When someone sends in an idea, I don't often respond because the idea is either terrible, I've already done it or they sue if I use it. Several years ago, I was coming up to my office in the elevator on a rainy day. Everyone was dripping and one young woman said, "You ought to do a piece on umbrellas."

I did a piece on umbrellas and that's the last time I recall taking a suggestion from anyone. (The basic problem with umbrellas is, the handle is right in the middle where you want to stand to stay dry.)

All that stuff of yours is good but it's a written piece, not for television. Years ago I did an hour for Harry Reasoner called "The Strange Case of the English Language." It was fun for me and reasonably successful but the number of people who care about the niceties of usage don't make a large television audience.

Two weeks ago I took a piece to Hewitt on the subject of the ways we write our alphabet. Handwritten letters are hard to read because there are too many different ways to form our letters. The small "r" is easily mistaken for an "n." Capital "D" or capital "R" are ridiculous letters when written with all the flourishes so many people use. Don hated the idea.

For years, when I write letters, I've dropped the apostrophes from words that are unmistakable without them but I can't get a publisher to go along with it in a book. "Dont," "isnt," "arent," "wont," "wasnt." It's hard to be consistent though because you need the apostrophe in "she's," "we're" etc.

While there isn't usually as much excuse for excess verbiage in a written piece, some fat is understandable and even necessary in spoken English. We all speak faster than people can listen and there has to be some padding in the language to give people time to hear—and ourselves time to get the next thought ready before we say it. Clichés are useful for that purpose, too.

But thanks. I really did like your ideas.

. . .

Kelly G. Ross
Redwood City, California

Dear Kelly,

A letter from the co-pilot of the B17 on which I flew on the raid over Wilhelmshaven, German, February 23, 1943, complaining about what I said about recreational vehicles, was not what I was looking for in today's mail.

It was great to hear from you, Kelly, in spite of your complaint about my opinions regarding the proliferation of RV's and trailer homes on our highways and in our open fields.

For the past year I've been contacting people I'd met during the war for a book I've just finished called *My War*. I wish I'd talked to you. We were together, perhaps eight feet apart for just seven hours of our lives and we didn't talk much then. I knew your last name but had not tried to locate you. I knew Casey was dead. I've talked to Wilson Elliot, Harold Lightbown and two or three other members of the *Banshee* crew. I gather you left Casey and the *Banshee* crew and you were pilot of your own B17 when you were shot down.

I had what I thought was quite an experience that day over Wilhelmshaven although I'm not sure you people upstairs in the cabin above us thought it was much. I know you had your hands full with your own problems. When a piece of flak picked off a six-inch piece of the plexiglass nose of the *Banshee*, the navigator whose name I don't have, went bonkers. I think it was his first trip and, in an effort to stop the freezing rush of air coming in through the jagged hole, he took off his gloves so he could stuff pieces of clothing in the hole. I looked across at Owens, the navigator, and he was slumped over his desk because his oxygen line had been cut. I spoke to Casey and he told me to take some oxygen in my lungs then take off my mask and come back up behind you guys and get a spare oxygen bottle. I was afraid I'd pass out for lack of oxygen but I got back with the bottle okay then hooked up Owens' mask and he regained consciousness almost immediately. Owens took over and got the navigator settled down.

We had our own little war down there and I think you and Casey were oblivious to it.

Now, about recreational vehicles. I'm sorry, yes I dislike them. I think they're a blight on the landscape. I understand everything you say but when you bring up your right to park one in *your* driveway in a fairly close neighborhood situation, you're ignoring the fact that your driveway and what it looks like, makes a difference to the appearance of the whole neighborhood. The idea that a man's home is his castle ends when his castle intrudes on my life and has an adverse effect on it.

Years ago I was with Barry Goldwater when we passed a community of what are called "mobile homes."

"If they're mobile" Barry snorted "why don't they move!" He proposed an ordinance for Arizona that required a mobile home to be moved at least twice a year. I realize you aren't talking about mobile homes but in the minds of many people, they are cousins to RVs.

Sorry about this. I am a great admirer of anyone who did what you did in the war. Eighth Air Force pilots were the best of the best. I ended up going on four bombing missions—two B17 missions, the one with the 306th, another with the 385th and two missions with the B26s over sub pens in France. The B26 trips were a walk in the park.

It would be good to see you. If you ever come to New York, I wish you'd call me and I'll buy lunch or dinner. You can park your RV out front—if you can find three empty parking places all together on a street in New York City.

. . .

Jack L. Trice
Portland, Maine

Dear Mr. Trice,

Thank you for the information on both windchill and degree days but I am still not absolutely persuaded that "windchill" isn't most often used by television weathermen to make weather sound more dramatic than it is some days.

With a camera crew, I taped the parking scene at several busy stores and was critical of the fact that people who were not handicapped used a lot of the spaces reserved for them. I was also critical of the fact that, too often, more spaces were set aside for the handicapped than was necessary.

I got a lot of critical mail.

Amy J. Taylor
Accent on Living Magazine
Bloomington, Illinois

Dear Ms. Taylor,

Several years ago, after watching with amazement as a blind man made his way alone through midtown New York, I contemplated covering my eyes, as though blind, and trying to duplicate his feat with a camera following me as a piece for television.

Thinking it over, we all decided it would seem more like a publicity stunt than a legitimate report so we abandoned the idea. Your suggestion of following someone in a wheelchair is too close to the same thing even though your purpose is to bring attention to their problems.

My enthusiasm for the Disabilities Act is unbounded. I'm proud of my Country when I see someone rolling down the street in a wheelchair where he or she could not have rolled just a few years ago.

I am less enthusiastic about a nine story building—the one I work in—which holds eighteen bathrooms, nine for men, nine for women—with thirty-six toilet stalls, eighteen of which are designed for use by the disabled even though there is not one person in the building whose special disability calls for the use of the kind of access that these facilities provide. Their design is for use by those with relatively rare disabilities.

Every time we spend money on one thing, we take it from another. It would be great to spend endless amounts of money on the physically disabled but if we do, we spend less on the deaf, the blind, on finding the secret of cancer and the answer to AIDS.

There is often conflict between those variously disabled, too. The blind, walking the streets with nothing but a cane with which to feel their way along, greatly dislike the street intersections where the curb has been moved and made into a sloping ramp for wheelchairs because their cane cannot tell them that they are about to cross a street.

With parking spaces for the disabled, there are very few people who would not approve of being inconvenienced in order to allow someone disabled to park closer to a store. There is, however, a certain amount of grumbling among the abled when there is no space available for them but ten empty spaces labeled HANDICAPPED which have never been used since the facility was built.

This does not suggest to me, as it did to you, that I have a hard-hearted attitude toward the disabled.

One man we photographed seemed physically able when he got out of the car he parked in a handicapped space. A week later, we got a letter from a lawyer threatening a lawsuit on his behalf. CBS lawyers wrote back asking for a doctor's verification of the man's handicapped status. We never heard back

. . .

In about 1978, shortly after I started doing regular essays on 60 Minutes, *I began getting more mail than I could read, let alone answer. I wrote a form letter that has been sent to hundreds of thousands of people.*

Memo to Letter Writers from Andy Rooney,

There are good things and bad things about this recent well-knownness of mine. The money's good but there are problems. One of the problems is mail. I simply don't know what to do about it. I hate to think of all the people I've offended by not answering a letter they've sent me but I'm often getting as many as 300 letters a day. I dislike answering letters but even if I liked doing it, I couldn't answer 300 a day and do anything else.

This may be the most formless form letter you ever got but I'll tell you something I've thought about my mail for a couple of years now. We all make friends in different sections of our lives. We make them in grade school, high school and maybe college. We graduate, get married, take a job or move to another town and we make a whole new group of friends. We still like our old friends but our paths have diverged and we lose each other. We don't see our good old friends anymore. We make new friends and eventually part with them too. Our lives are compartmented and we have different friends in each compartment. No one can be friends all the time with all the friends he or she has made. Very often we lose track of them completely and can't even send them a Christmas card.

One of the best things about being in the public eye—and, believe me, there aren't many good things about it—is that my old friends can find me and write me. Them I write back. Everyone else who writes me a good letter makes me feel terrible because I have to send them this.

Forgive me,

(signed Andy Rooney)

Every night, when I get home, I sit in my chair, watching the news on television and throwing away eight or ten, stamped, self-addressed envelopes from people who want an autograph or a signed picture. Throwing them away makes me feel bad but not as bad as sending an autographed picture of myself would make me feel.

Dear Eleanor Mahoney,

This is in response to your letter asking for my autograph. I don't sign my name on a sheet of paper for people who ask me to do that and for some reason, your letter has moved me to try to say why.

If you're going to succeed, you have to have confidence in yourself and it's difficult to be confident without being too confident. It amuses me to think that my appraisal of myself is close to what it ought to be. I'm not egotistical but I'm not especially modest.

It's best if you can count out what other people say they think of you. Everyone wants people to like them and, generally speaking, we all try to make friends with everyone we meet. We hope they overestimate us. We don't want them to have an accurate opinion of us. We want them to have a better opinion of us than we deserve. That's why we smile even though nothing strikes us funny and we praise them even if they haven't done much to deserve it. We tell stories about ourselves that make us look good and skip the ones that make us look bad.

All that may be okay but if we succeed in making people think more highly of us than we deserve, it's best if we, at least, don't take their elevated opinion of us seriously.

I'm recognizable to a lot of people and they write me for my autograph, as you have, because of my regular appearance on television.

I hope you'll excuse me for saying that people everywhere, but Americans in particular, have this dumb way of equating celebrity with excellence, competence and intelligence in everything.

Those attributes don't have much to do with being well known. The well-known person usually knows how to do one thing well but he or she is not necessarily a wonderful or exceptionally smart person because of it.

I've almost certainly given a lot of people the impression I'm a conceited jerk because I won't write my name on the card or piece of paper that they push at me on the street or in a restaurant.

I was thinking I ought to be clear in my own mind why I won't give my autograph. To begin with, if it's important to make an accurate appraisal of yourself, it's certainly best if you make that appraisal without any help from outside. You shouldn't put much faith in what other people think of your ability—and that goes both ways, too. You shouldn't get thinking you're better than you are because other people think you're good and you shouldn't get depressed when other people have a low opinion of your ability. You ought to decide for yourself.

Just as soon as I write my name on a piece of paper, I'm agreeing with the person who asks for it that I'm a wonderful person whose autograph is worth saving. This is nonsense and I refuse to be put in that embarrassing position. When you ask me for my autograph you are demeaning yourself and forcing more esteem on me than I'm worth.

At least I'm going to use your stamped envelope to send you this letter instead of throwing it way.

. . .

Ten percent of all the letters I get is nut mail. Every once in a while it amuses me to waste time answering it.

Ms. Debby Pangloss
Arlington, Virginia

Dear Ms. Pangloss,

Thank you for your letter. I was interested to hear that you have additional information on the Rodney King case that was withheld.

Please get it to me as soon as possible, with information about your source. I can assure you that if it is something we missed, it will be broadcast.

Overnight mail will reach me the following day. I await your letter with the additional information.

Dear Mr. Brainard,

While idling away the hours before the Super Bowl game I came across your good letter complaining about my treatment of triangles.

I do understand the importance of the triangle.

I did not say, as you quote me as saying that, "triangles have little use in the real world."

I did say that, considering what a good word "isosceles" is and how frequently it's used in school in geometry classes, "isosceles" doesn't come up very often in real life."

I was speaking more about language than form.

Dear Jim,

Yes, thanks.

People are always advising me to sue. Yesterday we were driving to Rensselaerville and we stopped for gas at a self-serve place near Saugerties. As I put the nozzle back in its holder, an interesting looking guy with a sports car and an attractive wife said "Hey, Andy Rooney, I've always wanted to meet you. My wife works for a woman named Andy Rooney."

"Ande Rooney," A-N-D-E, makes an assortment of kitschy refrigerator door magnets and other attractive trinkets and the idea of suing her for using an approximation of my name has often occurred to me.

It turned out this woman works for someone whose name has been Ande Rooney all her life. Her husband's name is Peter Rooney. She's been making those things for fifteen years.

So much for getting rich by suing her for using my name.

Dear Mrs. Clark,

The feeling in our house was that a name was meant to make it easy to identify a person and separate that person from others. For that reason we never named any of our children "after" anyone else in the family. We don't, for instance, have another Andrew . . . so I'm pleased that you've named a son after me. Or, at least, I'm not displeased. Or, anyway, I'm not displeased as I'd be over a lot of other things you might have done with my name.

Andrew is a good name no matter what reason you gave it to your son. I'm not much taken with Andy but I'm stuck with it and it doesn't bother me. My wife, a few friends and relatives call me Andrew but some good friends and relatives call me Andy, too. A nickname isn't the choice of the person who has it.

This is the best I can do by way of giving you something to glue in your son's memory book. Keep in mind that by the time he's old enough to care, I won't be anyone he's ever heard of.

Sincerely,

Andrew Aitken Rooney

Margaret Schulz
Osoyoos, British Columbia

Dear Margaret,

Thank you for writing. You're the best friend I ever had in Osoyoos.
Sincerely,
Andrew A. Rooney

. . .

Ralph D. Brandewiede
Auburn, Maine

Dear Mr. Brandewiede,

You win with your contention that Maine is a great place to live. I think the American public would rank it in the top five among their favorite states. It's surprising, in view of this, that so few people have chosen to live there—which, of course, is part of Maine's charm.

. . .

Mr. Luc S. Forest
Lorraine (Quebec) Canada

Dear Luc,

What's with "Lorraine (Quebec)"? It makes Lorraine sound like another name for Quebec.

I'm pleased you wrote but I can't tell you how much I appreciate your not having called yourself to my attention in the men's room in the service area along Route #87 where we had both stopped.

I usually pull a cap down over my eyes, seeking anonymity but from the results I get, that apparently only makes me look like Andy Rooney with a cap pulled down over his eyes.

Enjoyed your letter.

. . .

Lois Rodabaugh
Tabor, Iowa

Dear Lois,

I still want to tour the Country in a Rolls Royce, no matter what you say and I'd certainly come through Iowa. While I agree there aren't many places along back roads to get a Rolls fixed, they don't break down.

I spent three weeks in Humboldt, Harry Reasoner's hometown, doing a one hour documentary called "A Small Town In Iowa," so I know a little about Iowa. The people in Humboldt were proud that there was no liquor store there—but there was no bookstore, either.

. . .

Almost everyone who writes wants something but it's not always clear what they want.

"I hope to turn a sixty acre farm north of Forrest City, Arkansas, into a place where people over fifty-five can live and work together" writes Sarah Lange. "Being a realistic person, I know this can't be done by myself alone, so I am inviting you to share in my endeavor. Time, knowledge and money are needed" she writes and concludes by asking God to bless me for my kindness.

Dear Sarah,

For the time being, until I know more about your project, hold off on asking God to bless me for my kindness because I haven't decided yet whether to be kind to you or not.

It has a sort of Whitewater sound to it and I suspect you'd rather have my money than my time or knowledge.

. . .

Marion Smith Collins
Calhoun, Georgia

Dear Ms. Collins,

Your book sounds good but I don't agree with you about organizing a home library. A good home library doesn't have to be organized. You know your books and pretty much know where they are. Anyway, most people don't decide what they want to read and then look in their file catalog for it. Something catches their eye and they take it off the shelf. That's the way a home library should work.

If I were advising anyone on assembling a library, I'd advise them against it. Books collect plenty fast without anyone having to be a book-collector and going at it deliberately. The word "assemble" itself is not right. By the time you get to be about fifty, the problem is more one of weeding out books than acquiring them. Bookshelves need as much weeding as a garden and the weeds are not so apparent.

My advice—I know you didn't ask me for it—is as follows:

1. Don't buy any fiction unless it's one of the old classics.
2. Don't buy any tall books.

3. Keep books you're sure you like and want to have even if you know you'll never read them again.
4. Don't hesitate to deface books in your own collection by writing in the margins and on the blank pages in front and back. That's the difference between your books and a library's.
5. When you build the bookshelves they need only be 7" deep but you should have an equal number of shelves 9" and 11" high. Things like dictionaries don't fit on a shelf 7" high. The bottom shelf should be 13". If a book is taller than that, lay it flat.

. . .

Carol Starr is a practicing astrologist in California whose husband is a dentist. She wrote to defend astrology.

Carol Starr,
Paradise Valley, California

Dear Carol,

Your letter was so nice I can hardly help liking you but I detest everything about astrology. I believe in astrology about as much as your dentist husband believes in the tooth fairy.

Astrology appeals to the least educated among us and they are the people who can least afford to indulge in such nonsense. It appeals to them because it allows them to fool themselves into thinking they can substitute hopes and dreams and predestination for work and clear thinking. It relieves them of the necessity most of us feel to think things through clearly and logically and act in our best interests according to the facts.

Write and tell me you've turned to Palmistry, Tarot Cards or become a Hari Krishna—anything but astrology. If you do this for me I will intercede with God and ask him to see to it that people have enough serious problems with their teeth in Paradise Valley so that your husband will be able to support you in the manner to which astrology has made you accustomed.

. . .

For twenty-five years I've used a calendar on which all the days of the week are on the same line across. The dates go down, column-style. It was developed by a Boston clergyman named Phillips Brooks in the 1800s and I am so used to it, I can't use any other calendar. When the company that made them in Boston went out of business in about 1988, I wrote about it. A Florida businessman and horse breeder named Harry Mangurian was in the same fix and for the past ten years, he has made or had made—the Phillips Brooks-style calendar. They are beautifully done on heavy cardboard, usually with a picture of one of his prize stallions on the cover. His wife, Dotty always sends me several.

Mrs. Harry Mangurian
Mockingbird Farm
Ocala, Florida

Dear Dottie,

Thanks once more for the Phillips Brooks calendars ("so called because this was the style used by him"). Tell Harry I'd be lost without mine.

He might also like to know that his calendars have been particularly useful for me during IRS audits. Anything you can do to confuse an auditor is all to the good and when a tax man tries to follow an itinerary of mine by studying my Brooks-style calendar, he often gets lost or discouraged.

Don Sauers
Lancaster, Pennsylvania

Dear Mr. Sauers,

Thank you for *Time For America*, your book chronicling the saga of the Hamilton watch. They've been one of the good things about America. I don't carry my old Hamilton railroad watch, I hang it from a small brass nail on the bookcase next to my chair in the living room. It's easy to remember to wind it there. We all need some easy jobs we're confident we know how to do every day and I know how to shave and wind my watch.

I read an ad for a Swiss watch in a London newspaper that said "not quartz since 1792 and never quartz."

As part of the old fogey generation, I fight progress on every hand myself but how in the world can they make a spring fed watch that will run as accurately as even the cheapest quartz watch? The quartz watch is one of the most significant inventions of the 20th Century—on a par with the elastic band and television remote control. They keep exact time and are trouble free. I wear one that cost me $27.

I've been given several watches now just for being old. CBS gave me one after I'd been there thirty-five years and *60 Minutes* gave me one for twenty-five. They're both attractive, expensive watches but neither is satisfactory because one has a sweep hand and fancy little marks on the dial instead of numbers. The other has numbers but no sweep hand.

Even though I know where "3" is on a watch, I don't want anything clever on the face of it indicating the hours. I still want numbers to reassure me. I like a sweep hand because I'm always timing how long it takes me to do something. It takes me nine seconds to climb the seventeen stairs in our house. The elevator from the first to the seventh floor at CBS takes thirty-seven seconds. One stop adds nine seconds.

Thanks again for your book.

Doctors write a lot of letters. They frequently point out some life-threatening problem they diagnose by observing me on television.

Dear Dr. Lessing,

Yes, I'm aware that my left hand is not steady when I hold something up to the camera with it. Someone told me I had "essential tremor," not Parkinson's.

Let me ask you a question: Is the life-expectancy of doctors any higher than that of lawyers? If it isn't, doctors either have a credibility problem or they aren't taking their own advice.

. . .

James Miller
Dodge City, Iowa

Dear Jim,

I'm always happy to hear from someone in Dodge City although naturally I'd prefer the letter fawned over my talent more than yours did. Yours hardly did at all, when you come right down to it.

While I admire the poetic naturc of your statement "Beauty signifies the entire quality of a person," I'm not looking for entire quality when I tune in to watch the Miss America contest. And I don't think a pretty girl is like a melody, either.

If I ever need a lawyer in Dodge City, I hope we can swallow our differences and work together.

A man named Ty M. Sparks wrote to say the Postal Service demanded unnecessarily long addresses on envelopes. He suggested I write him with nothing but his box number and zip code.

May 23, 1993

TMS
1178
79014

Dear Ty,
Just checking to see if it works.
Sincerely,
Andrew A. Rooney

The other I gave his full address.

Ty M. Sparks
112 Main St.
PO Drawer 1178
Canadian, Texas 79014–1178

Dear Ty,
Just checking to see if it works.
Sincerely,
Andrew A. Rooney

Ty received both letters.

Dear Mr. Berklin,

We all know car dealers have to make a living and we're willing to have you make a profit but we are not willing to pay more than the lowest price you can sell for and still make that profit.

Too many car dealers run their businesses as though they were Turkish carpet salesmen on a street in Ankara. We all know now that the sticker price on the side window of a car in a showroom has nothing to do with what a dealer will end up selling it for. Other businesses don't work that way in America. How come?

In addition, it's apparent that manufacturers intentionally muddle prices with a wide variety of "options" which make prices difficult to compare. And, of course, half the time, you can't buy the car *without* the "optional equipment." What kind of an option is that?

There used to be something amusing about the adversarial relationship between car buyer and car seller but it isn't so funny anymore.

My friend Bob Forte went into a showroom in Charleston and sat down in front of a desk with a salesman behind it. They haggled and the salesman offered a price that Bob still thought was a thousand dollars too high . . . At a strategic moment, the sales manager came along and asked how things were going.

He asked what price the salesman had offered and when he told him, the manager feigned rage.

"You have no authority to offer a price like that" he yelled at the salesman.

"You actually made him that offer?"

"I did" the salesman said.

"Well, okay then" the manager said "we'll stand by our promise but after this you have to check with me."

It was obviously a con game they had played a thousand times with customers. It was more like the midway at a carnival than an automobile showroom.

I heard of another dealer who had hidden microphones in the salesman's office. After a man and his wife dickered with the salesman, he would offer some excuse and leave the room. While the potential buyers talked about how much they could actually pay, the manager and the salesman listened in and fixed their price according to what they'd heard.

Buying a new car is one of life's delights and dealers shouldn't be taking the pleasure out of it for us.

. . .

Francis Underhill
Flat Rock, North Carolina

Dear Francis,

I wish you hadn't sent me your column. You did it better than I did!

You might be amused at a phenomenon I've noted. I get more mail per reader from the papers I have in North Carolina than from any other state. You might conclude, as a North Carolinian, that it's because the people of North Carolina are more literate that the people of other states but if that's true, how do you account for the election of Jesse Helms as senator?

John D.G. Dormer
San Diego, California

Dear John,

Thanks for your offer to initiate a campaign for the Presidency on my behalf.

I'd take you up on it but I like to mow my own lawn. There are eighteen acres around the White House and if I lived there, I wouldn't have time to do anything else.

PART FOUR

Dear Editor

A great American custom is writing a usually angry letter-to-the-editor. I have frequently been moved to write one. Editors, most often, have not been impressed enough with whatever I've been angry enough to write about, to run it. Not having your letter printed is another American custom.

To the Editor,

Dr. Donald Mender writes (May 5, 1997) "It seems likely that some variant of the Penrose paradigm, bringing together nonlinear and self-referent properties of our minds, will ultimately prevail." In so saying, Dr. Mender took the words right out of my mouth. I spoke with two friends whose mouths Dr. Mender also took the words right out of.

To the Editor, *The New York Times,*

A brief notice today on page 12 read "Because of Ascension Thursday, alternate side street parking rules will be suspended."

Might not a more thorough treatment of this matter be in order? Readers might be interested in knowing the following:

How many New Yorkers regularly celebrate Ascension Thursday?

How many get Ascension Thursday off?

What is a typical Ascension Thursday holiday meal? Pierre Franey might provide us with some tips on how to prepare an Ascension Thursday dinner.

Does the Bible refer to alternate side parking?

A reporter might also be able to ascertain whether or not this is some fake Sanitation Department reason for suspending alternate side parking having to do with its union.

To the Editor, *The New York Times,*

The question raised in *The Times* about why there are relatively few Stars of David over the graves of American soldiers in the military cemetery at Colleville above Omaha Beach, is overshadowed by the fact that those two religious symbols, the cross and the star, are the *only* markers. There is not one grave identifying its fallen soldier as none-of-the-above.

If I had been killed in Normandy, a not unlikely possibility, my grave would have erroneously indicated that I was Christian or Jewish and I am neither.

There must have been others like me.

. . .

The following is an unpublished Letter-To-The-Editor of The New York Times *following a story about the problems doctors were having with lawsuits.*

To the Editor,

The whole malpractice issue might be resolved if doctors treated any lawyer with a serious illness on a contingency basis.

If the lawyer lived, he'd have to pay the doctor. If he died, he wouldn't have to pay.

The Times *in London didn't run what I wrote as an op-ed piece for them, either.*

To the Editor, *The Times*, London, England

For four years of my life I was a reporter for the Army newspaper, *The Stars and Stripes*, and for two of those years I worked in your building on Printing House Square. There may still be a pressman around who remembers us.

Our daughter, Ellen, was working for ABC News in London several years ago and she met an Englishman, married him and now lives there. We talk frequently on the phone and exchange clippings we think might be of interest. Yesterday I received from her a long obituary of Donald Swann, the piano-playing partner of the great British comedy team of Flanders and Swann, which had been printed in your paper.

Everyone older than forty in the United States remembers them from television here and from their long-running show on Broadway called *At the Drop of a Hat.* They were very popular in the United States.

The obituary you printed has no byline so I don't know who wrote it. Anything this long in a newspaper and with so many personal opinions in it ought to be signed. A reader should know who's saying these things. A writer ought to have to own up to his work.

I'm familiar with the fact that there is a fair amount of anti-Americanism in Great Britain. I don't know whether it's resentment over our relative success during the time the British Empire has been falling apart or what it is but it's there and it's often insidious. Insidious is the word for what the anti-Americanism is in this obituary of Donald Swann.

Three quarters of the way through the article, the writer says Flanders and Swann came to New York.

"American audiences, when they first encountered the pair in 1959, hardly knew what to make of them. 'An over-age altar boy who is losing his hair' began the *Herald Tribune*'s bewildered critic on Swann."

Well . . . the critic, Walter Kerr, one of the best theater critics there ever was in either of our countries, was not bewildered at all and neither is that the start of his review.

"At the Drop of a Hat . . . has no scenery, no costumes, no orchestra—just two men alone on stage completely surrounded by talent." That's how Kerr's review began.

Does that sound as though the New York critic "hardly knew what to make of them"? Why would a London writer say that?

It seems likely that the writer said that because he never considered the possibility that an old American like me has a daughter in London who would send him that obituary and that I, in turn, would bother to look back into the files to read exactly what the *Herald Tribune* critic *did* say.

This reporter not only checked that October 9, 1959 *Herald Tribune*, he read the reviews of *At the Drop of a Hat* in four other New York newspapers that existed at the time and found they were all wildly favorable.

In the *New York Times*, Brooks Atkinson said "Most people in the Golden Theater last night seemed to be thoroughly delighted . . . "

Walter Kerr ended his review in the *Herald Tribune* by saying "Whatever it is that runs through these gentlemen's veins, it makes them lively, witty, literate, ingratiating, explosively funny and excellent, excellent, companions for a daffy and delightful evening."

Why would a *Times* writer of an obituary go so far out of his way to contribute, with deliberate untruths, to the popular British idea that Americans don't get it?

PART FIVE

About the War

As a sophomore at Colgate University, I became interested in the ideas of an economics professor named Kenneth Boulding. I was not so much interested in his economic theories as in his philosophy of life which seemed profound to me at the time. He stammered badly and that gave weight to his opinions.

The Nazis were in the process of taking over Europe and, although the United States had not yet entered the war, it was arming and preparing a civilian draft in anticipation of that probability.

In his classes, Boulding taught very little economics but expounded his theory of pacifism. "Any peace is better than any war" rang in my ears, although I later learned it was borrowed from Plato.

Everyone in the class had to register for the draft and, under Boulding's influence, I contemplated registering as a "Conscientious Objector" and refusing to serve. I spent an agonizing three months anticipating going to prison if I refused.

More from weakness and fear than from conviction, I reluctantly registered and was drafted at the end of my junior year in August of 1941. Two and a half years later, on April 12th, 1944, I entered the concentration camp at Buchenwald. It was the most [illegible] day my self-esteem ever suffered because I realized, finally, what an idiot I had been. I wanted to take Ken Boulding by his pacifist hand and lead him past the horror of what I witnessed.

When I wrote about this recently, I was surprised that so many people knew of Kenneth Boulding.

Edward F. Snyder
Bar Harbor, Maine

Dear Mr. Snyder,

Thank you for the copy of *There Is a Spirit* by Kenneth Boulding.

I knew Boulding well in college and kept track of where he was afterwards. I wrote him in Colorado about a year ago because I thought he might have heard of me—although he may not have—and wondered whether he recalled having me as a student. I wanted to tell him, too, how I felt now about how he had influenced me into thinking I was a pacifist. I did not write in an unfriendly way because I still admired him. I never heard back and assumed he was not well enough to reply.

I never understood Boulding's brilliance as an economist. I believed it but had never seen any direct evidence of it that I could comprehend.

In retrospect, I think he was more of a well . . . a religious nut. He was certainly an extraordinarily decent human being but I've grown intolerant of religious nuts, even decent ones.

His booklet of black poems with its foreword, preface and introduction, seems pretentious. I'm glad to have it and I'll go back at it but I took little from a first reading. I'm willing to accept the possibility this is my shortcoming, not the poems' but I don't even seem to know why they're called *The Naylor Sonnets*. (The best line I read was Naylor's "There is a spirit which I feel that delights to do no evil . . . ." It reminded me of something Charles Kuralt wrote for print several years ago after years of travelling across the Country. It began "There is in this Country, a conspiracy among good people to do good things.")

Anyone who decides to write poetry, should first master prose. I have not read enough of Ken Boulding's prose to know whether or not he had a license to write obscurant verse.

Merrill Barnebey
Ashland, Oregon

Dear Mr. Barneby,

Thank you for Leonard Silk's book about Kenneth Boulding.

The date of Boulding's vision of Christ, May 15, 1940, as described, was a surprise to me because it was during that period that I knew him. Funny he didn't mention it at the time. I'd remember because I would have asked "What do you mean you SAW Christ suffering on the cross when you got out of the bathtub? You mean you saw a vision of Christ? What's a vision? You imagined you saw him? How long had you been in the tub? What DO you mean?"

Silk doesn't make it clear when Boulding wrote "I feel hate rising in my throat . . . ." The implication is that he wrote it before May 15, 1940. I doubt that. From what I knew of him, it must have been written after 1941. His pacifism and refusal to hate had not yet been undermined when I left him in the last days of May 1941.

It all seems like nonsense to me. The more I read of Boulding's pretentious poetry, the less respect I have for his intellect. I'm beginning to suspect he was not the intellectual giant I took him to be as an impressionable college student.

I am embarrassed to have been taken in by him.

Henry M. Burman
State College, Pennsylvania

Dear Hank,

Your letter reminded me that for all the bad things about the war, there were a surprising number of good things that will never be matched in peacetime.

Some of the actions the B17 crews took after they'd been hit were braver than the action of Sergeant York. Looking through some old newspapers, I came on a story I wrote about a B17 pilot named Raymond Cheek, who had died at the controls over the target in Germany after taking a direct hit to his head from an FW 190 machine gun bullet. My story was about the valiant co-pilot, Bill Cassedy, who brought the bomber home sitting next to his dead friend.

As I read the story I'd written fifty years ago, I was pleased with myself for having done what seemed like a competent job of reporting. I decided to call around to see how many of the crew whose names I had included, I could find alive today.

What I discovered by talking to one of the men who had been on board, Milton Blanchette, was a shock to me. I had completely missed the most dramatic element of the story I had been so proud of.

Bill Cassedy, had brought the plane back and landed at the base with the wind at his tail, something an experienced pilot would never do. I never asked why.

Cassedy died a few years ago but Milton Blanchette, the top turret gunner, told me what I had never known. He said Raymond Cheek was to have been married to a nurse on the base the following day and friends at the base had arranged a party for him and his bride-to-be. The party was to have taken place on the runway when Cheek finished his twenty-fifth mission and rolled to a triumphant stop. Cassedy couldn't stand the thought of bringing the B17 in and coming to a halt in front of the welcoming committee, including his bride-to-be, with Ray Cheek slumped in the pilot's seat in a pool of blood with his head blown off. He decided to risk landing the damaged plane with the wind at its tail so Ray Cheek's friend who was so much in love with him, would never see what had happened.

You don't get a lot of heroes like Bill Cassedy in peacetime.

. . .

In any war, there's always a rumor about a great new weapon that's going to end it. One of those in WW II was a sophisticated bombsight installed in B17s and B24s, which could be calibrated to take into effect the speed of the aircraft, height, distance to the target and windspeed. It had to be done quickly close to the target and many of our young bombardiers were not able to use it effectively.

I wrote as much and had to answer a lot of complaints.

Dear Mr. Houser,

I was interested to learn you flew out of Molesworth with the 303rd Bomb Group but was unimpressed by your defense of the Norden bombsight. If it had been any good, it would not have been necessary to destroy German cities and kill hundreds of thousands of women and children to get at a legitimate military target. Of course our bombing and that of the RAF helped end the war. That has nothing to do with the inadequacy of the bombsight.

You say you were a bombardier. Did you actually use the Norden bombsight? If you did you must have flown with the lead plane, perhaps with Gen. Curtis LeMay, because after a few abortive attempts made to let each bombardier operate independently, the 8th Air Force gave up. Subsequently the trailing B17s released their bombs on cue from the lead aircraft, not at the discretion of the bombardier in the individual B17s.

. . .

The subject of bravery has always interested me partly because the word has been used too loosely and partly because of my curiosity about whether I had the quality myself or not. In looking over old letters, I was surprised by how often the subject came up.

Dear Mrs. Grimm,

Your good letter moved me. Your husband was one of quite a few people who served in our armed forces with a special dedication not shared by all or even a majority of our peacetime soldiers and sailors.

The Pentagon is a nest swarming with military people who are afraid or incapable of making it out in the unprotected world. And I'm perfectly aware that there are many able and dedicated people there too, but they are not a majority. The majority of officers in the Pentagon is waiting for its pension.

As much as I liked your letter, I must tell you that I object to the use of the word "brave" in relation to every soldier and sailor who ever served. They are people like the rest of us and many of them have taken refuge in the armed forces. Bravery comes up infrequently in war and, when it's called for, not everyone in the armed forces answers.

I do not think that being in our armed forces entitles a man or woman to be labeled "brave."

From your description, I think I understand the type of sailor your husband was and he deserves our great admiration. Not all do.

Alexander H. Hadden
Grafton, Vermont

Dear Sandy,

As much as I agree with some of your statements about infantrymen, I don't agree with your contention that the absence of cowardice is heroism. Cowardice would be turning and running which wasn't an option for an infantryman. And where do you put fear in the mix? A lack of fear isn't heroism, either. It was more often stoicism in someone's genes or a failure to envision or comprehend danger. A lot of guys I saw who weren't afraid had faulty synapses (if that's the word I need). They didn't relate danger to the imminence of death. They were not cowardly but neither were they brave and it is, as you say, what won the war for us. But I'd prefer to reserve the word brave for more special cases like when a man knowingly risked his life to do a good thing for someone else.

It would be good to see you again at which time we could bore the other guests in the room by continuing this dialog about our war.

. . .

Richard C. Hottelet
Wilton, Connecticut

Dear Dick,

You can help me if you have time. I've been working for more than two years on a book to be called *My War*. I have been irritated over the years by the use, in books about the war, of that literary device, the synthetic particular as in, ". . . de Gaulle occupied himself that night reading from a leatherbound edition of Moliere's *Le Bourgeois Gentihomme*." That was from *Is Paris Burning* by Collins and Lapierre. Now, who the hell knows what de Gaulle was reading alone that night? And "leather-bound"? I'm determined to avoid the device but it's so difficult to get the facts I can understand being tempted to use it.

I've written about the fight in the dining room of the small hotel in Rambouillet, outside Paris, between Hemingway and a Chicago news-man named Bruce Grant, the night of August 22, 1945.

We were all there for three nights waiting for the move into Paris and I cannot avoid telling about the fake story Charles Collingwood wrote detailing the fall of Paris. He wrote it well before Paris actually fell, based on his intimate knowledge of the city and somehow got the story to the CBS bureau in London.

While I don't suppose it's your favorite subject, Ed Murrow, as bureau chief there, had you read Collingwood's story on the air and it caused a great stir around the world. I hoped you could straighten me out on some of the details.

Charles was a respected CBS News correspondent and a good guy but a lot of reporters who were in Rambouillet before we got to Paris, never forgave him for that serious lapse in journalistic ethics. You were so totally innocent that it must have been difficult for you in later years to have been drawn into it.

Did his story arrive in London recorded on wire or written on paper? How did he get it from Rambouillet to London? What kind of a HOLD did he put on it? Did he indicate that it should not be broad-cast until Paris actually fell? What details did it give? What was your conversation with Ed Murrow about it? Did the censors ever see it?

Anything you can say about it would help.

Herman S. Wolk
Chief Historian
Center for Air Force History
Washington, D.C.

Dear Mr. Wolk,

I wish you had not told me about Geoffrey Perret. I bought both *There's a War To Be Won* and *Winged Victory* and they are daunting works of research and writing. The book I am writing, *My War*, is so much a personal account of my view of it that, fortunately for me, it cannot be compared to Geoffrey Perret's.

When I started as a reporter years ago, I was impressed with what dog work it was. Nothing glamorous about it. No major news story was ever revealed to me in a flash. I got one little bit of information and used it in my next interview to elicit yet another. And so it went, piling up one fact after another until I had a story. There were no scoops.

When I started the book, I was afraid most of my WW II sources were dead or suffering from Alzheimer's but one good source led to another and I have pages of phone numbers now of people who have first hand knowledge of the war I knew.

I do want to say something to you as a historian though: I am appalled at how infrequently the historical facts of the event I am writing about, concur with my memory of it. A primary objective of the Center for Air Force History should be to correct this and bring history into line with my recollection of it.

Joe Ornstein
Delray Beach, Florida

Dear Joe,

It wasn't clear to me whether you knew that Elwood Quesada died Feb 9th. I interviewed him for stories half a dozen times during the War. He was the ultimate, all-American fighter pilot, handsome, brave and dashing. Not a typical general.

When the P47s first came to the British Isles in 1943, it was big news although officially a secret until we were sure the Germans knew they were there. I went out to an airfield with a press group and they gave us a look at the plane with the understanding we were not to say the P47s had arrived until they told us we could.

We had a very knowledgeable editor and writer, a sergeant named Bud Hutton, who had collected every scrap of information ever written about the P47. The one rule the censors had was, if we could prove information about something had been in print before, *The Stars and Stripes* could run it. Bud put together all the facts he brought together from dozens of sources and wrote it into one, long, informative article about the P47 and the paper published it. I was the one in trouble, of course, because of my promise of silence. No one noticed that Bud never said the P47 was in England but his article practically assumed that.

The next day an official packet of papers arrived in Hutton's mailbox. It was an order from Gen. Hunter for court-martial proceedings to be instituted against us for violating a military secret.

Hutton, the sergeant editor, looked briefly at the papers, from the general, scribbled "DISAPPROVED, BH" in the top right-hand corner and sent them back to Hunter's office.

Nothing more was ever heard.

Ed Dowly, a friend of mine in London with the Signal Corps, planned to make the trip back to Normandy for the 50th anniversary of the D-Day Invasion. (I always capitalize that Invasion.) He wrote to say he looked forward to going but couldn't remember much about what was going on in the United States at the time.

Dear Ed,

When you wrote, I had been looking through my old *Stars and Stripes* files to bring myself up to date on the sort of thing you've forgotten because I've forgotten, too. Here are some notes I've made that should jog your memory. The old papers serve me almost like a diary and before we leave for Normandy, I was refreshing my own memory and looking for something that might make a feature piece for television while we are over there.

Here are my notes:

- British boy, 2, orphaned as mother tries to save U.S. crew in burning bomber.
- Two captains and a major shipped overseas shortly after they were married complain of "hardship" and want to be sent back to states. A chaplain tried to help them by quoting the bible to authorities:

  "When a man hath taken a new wife, he shall not go out to war . . . but he shall be free at home for one year and shall cheer up his wife which he hath taken." It didn't work.
- Siamese twins born to mother of 8th AF gunner killed over Germany.
- Otto Huttenen, of Warren, Ohio, blinded in North Africa is married to a British nurse . He is sent home just before all travel from British Isles, for any reason, is stopped.
- DOCTOR TELLS ROOSEVELT TO TAKE IT EASY.
- Americans are asked to eat more eggs because of an egg glut.

There are so many eggs that farmers are being paid only fifteen cents a dozen.

- Stamps are six cents.
- RED SKELTON DRAFTED. CLARK GABLE AND JIMMY STEWART ENLIST.
- Rita Hayworth is pictured kneeling on bed in black lace negligee.
- SAFE-CRACKERS GET RATION COUPONS FOR 2,000 SCARCE AUTOMOBILE TIRES, 4,500 PAIRS OF SHOES AND 100,000 GALLONS OF GAS.
- FURTHER TRAINING OF WOMEN PILOTS STIRRING A BATTLE IN AIR CORPS.
- Report of a coal shortage because all the miners have been drafted.
- Catholic priest named James Gillis tells league of Catholic Women that "Hollywood weddings, Reno divorces, jitterbugging and obscene literature are driving civilization back to the jungle."
- DRUMMER GENE KRUPA ARRESTED ON MARIJUANA CHARGE.
- Rhonda Fleming poses on the bed this time.
- 171,257 airplanes built in the United States since Pearl Harbor. 1,000 4-engine bombers being finished every month.
- Strike at Packard Motors plant.
- When one striking group was warned that it imperiled the Invasion, they went back to work.
- 80,000 landing craft built in 1943.
- 90,000 TONS OF CHEESE SENT TO ENGLAND.
- The U.S. Circuit Court rules that a separate Negro draft quota is not discriminatory.
- Lots of Frank Sinatra stories.

- 300 planes take off in an hour at Idlewild Airport in New York. That's before it was renamed Kennedy.
- TROOP SHIP SUNK IN MEDITERRANEAN. 498 MEN DROWN.
- ALLIED BOMBERS BLAST 36 RAIL TARGETS.
- Secretary of War Henry Stimson announces that there are 3,657,000 American soldiers in foreign countries now. The most ever.
- AIR POWER ALONE CANNOT WIN WAR.
- Gen. Omar Bradley says that losses won't be heavy on the day of the Invasion.
- Babe Didrikson called the best woman athlete of all time.
- Coach Lou Little of Columbia says pro football is ruining the college game.
- Ted Husing broadcast the Kentucky Derby.
- The boxers most often mentioned in the sports pages were Max Baer, Billy Conn, Jim Braddock and Joe Louis.
- Story says California boxing is corrupt.
- University of Arkansas beat City College of New York 39–37.
- MAN 70 KIDNAPS GIRL 14.
- A mailman who threw away a lot of mail instead of delivering it, claims he only threw away 2nd and 3rd class mail.
- Three boys on raft saved at the last minute from going over Niagara Falls.
- Winston Churchill, in the hospital, doesn't want to put down his cigar while being x-rayed.

I sent that to Ed Dowly in Chicago and looked for him during the Invasion ceremonies but never found him. I learned later that he died six weeks before his planned trip.

In 1995 I finished writing My War, *a book that was important to me because the war had been the biggest experience of my life. There were several factual errors in the book which were corrected when the paperback was published but, even though they were noted by only a few people, they were embarrassing. I said, for example, that The Flying Tigers flew P39s and every living member of The Flying Tigers wrote to tell me I was wrong. Their plane was the P40.*

I confused the two German rockets the V-1 and V-2 and referred to the 303rd Bomb Group when I should have said the 305th.

They may seem like small mistakes but not if you were with the Flying Tigers or one of those bomb groups and even one mistake damages the authenticity of a book.

In My War *I told the story of the ball turret gunner who had been trapped in his plastic bubble when his B17 was forced to land on its belly after the hydraulic system controlling the landing gear had been shot out. The mechanism designed to allow the ball turret gunner to rotate his bubble into a position where he could climb out and up into the B17, was jammed.*

I had written the story as a column years before and was surprised to find it turn up, after my column was published, as an episode in a series Steven Spielberg did for television. It was referred to in a skeptical review written for a Dallas newspaper by someone who, as I understood it, had read only the parts of My War *that an editor had faxed to him.*

Jim Frisinger
Letters Editor
The Dallas Morning News
Dallas, Texas

To The Editor,

As the author of *My War*, it would appeal to me if Philip Jennings saved up the money he spends on stamps for letters-to-the-editor and bought and read my book *My War* before he comments further on it. Having you fax him pages from it to criticize doesn't do anything for my income.

The incident mentioned in your review, which Mr. Jennings did read, took place at the airfield at Bassingbourne, England, where the 91st Bomb Group was stationed. The name of the ball turret gunner, crushed between the underside of the B17 and the tarmac, was withheld by censors at the time and I don't have it in my notes because I didn't know it. What happened was dramatic. To whom it happened is of no importance to anyone but his family and I'm not sure they'd want to know.

There are some mistakes in my book but the details of that story are not among them.

. . .

Jack Resen
El Paso, Texas

Dear Jack,

You're right about medals. Our military hands them out in such great numbers that most of them don't mean much. Honor to the genuine heroes who deserve them is less than it would be if they were not given so freely to so many who don't deserve them.

The two most idiotic medals and the ones we laughed at most during my four years in the Army were the ETO medal and the red, Good Conduct Medal. "ETO" stood for "European Theater of Operations" and anyone shipped there got an ETO medal even though being there was a choice the Army made for him. Anyone not actually in the guardhouse was eligible for the Good Conduct Medal.

Now, in Washington, you see thirty-five-year old lieutenant colonels around the Pentagon, too young to have served in any war, with four or five rows of ribbons on their chest. Each ribbon represents a medal or citation of some kind. On several occasions I have asked what the ribbons stand for and often the wearer can't identify all of them. They're as meaningless as jewelry.

A great deal of nonsense about bravery is perpetuated by the military. There are some things I don't say about it in public but the idea that every American soldier who served, was wounded, captured or killed was a hero is not true. I object because it diminishes the honor due genuine heroes.

I also wish major countries in the world would cut down on their displays of military pomp and power on state occasions. Why is that idiotic review-of-troops mandatory when a head-of-state visits another country? What's a "21-gun-salute" all about? What's a country trying to prove by having all those military people standing around in their medal-spangled uniforms? Is it "My father can beat your father"?

The display of military might in association with a state visit planned to promote peace, seems contradictory.

. . .

Henry H. Arnold, III
Eisenhower Army Medical Center
Fort Gordon, Georgia

Dear Major Arnold,

Those Army and Air Force leaders of WW II, like your father, were a fascinating group of men, often seriously flawed but all special in their own way. I met your father on a dozen occasions and he was one of the most special. His nickname "Hap" was fortuitous.

My book, *My War*, has not sold exceptionally well but it seems as though everyone who read it wrote me with some personal observation or anecdote pertaining to something in it.

I had a letter from a man whose father had been an aide to Gen. Frank Andrews, the 8th Air Force commander, and then to your father. He said his father had great respect for both men but, indicating how wrong a general could be, added that early in the war, when the B17s were first coming off the production line, your father said that if they built 500 of them, they probably wouldn't need any replacements. They built 12,761 B17s between 1942 and 1945 and 4,750 of them were shot down or otherwise destroyed in combat. Another 250 were lost in various accidents.

Your suggestion that I put together a book of my *Stars and Stripes* stories is interesting but I simply don't have the time or the enthusiasm for such a project. Some of the reports would stand up, some would not and I can't imagine that it would attract any readers except a fast-diminishing number of veterans of WW II.

Following up some of the people I wrote about by trying to find them now would be hard and discouraging work. When I came across several stories I'd written about Hubert Zemke, the great P47 pilot and squadron commander, I started to track him down in his hometown of Missoula, Montana. I found he'd moved to California. I got his address and phone number there. When I called, I learned that Hub Zemke had died the previous day.

There's just so much of that I could take.

. . .

I came away from WW II with a negative opinion of General George S. Patton and frequently spoke about it on television or wrote about it. Carlo D'Este is a good historian for whom I have great respect. He is author of Patton: A

Genius for War. *While writing the book he asked me for an opinion or any anecdote I had.*

Carlo W. D'Este
New Seabury, Massachusetts

Dear Mr. D'Este,

If it's a rational opinion of the man you're after, I'm not the person to give it. I detested Patton and everything about the way he was. It was because we had so few soldiers like him that we won the war.

A friend of mine, Bud Hutton, liked to say "The trouble with a peacetime Army is, in peacetime the enlisted men are no smarter than the officers."

Patton was the kind of officer that our wartime enlisted men were smarter than. It was the independent action of the average GI that made our Army so successful. Our success was not the result of the kind of blind, thoughtless devotion to the next higher authority that Patton lived by and demanded.

At a conference on military history at Cantigny, someone said, "Patton's role was crucial to success in Normandy." Success in Normandy? Patton wasn't in Normandy. I'm not sure where the border of Brittany and Normandy is but we were about out of Normandy when Patton's little Third Army was activated, a week after we took St. Lo. It was on August 1st. He took off then, presumably on orders, away from major elements of the German Army toward the submarine pens and other fortifications on the coast of Brittany. He then headed south. Of course he made good time. There was no one in front of him.

Have you made contact with Bill Mauldin? He has some good Patton stories although they are not so favorable to him as mine are. I'm sure you've talked to John Eisenhower. Patton was like an uncle to him.

John is very solid but he told me that he could not be critical of Patton because his father had entrusted him with command of the Third Army and to do so, would be critical of his father.

I hope your book will be about George Patton and not about George C. Scott. The real general spent too many American lives to buy glory for himself.

. . .

Mr. Neal P. Nelson
Lincoln, Nebraska

Dear Mr. Nelson,

Yes, I think George Patton was the most over-rated general of WW II. The broadcast you saw was well done in parts but seriously flawed in its choice of generals. Courtney Hodges was vastly more important to the conduct of the war in Europe than was Patton—as were others.

Both Eisenhower and Bradley, fine leaders in their own right, were soft on Patton because they had known him at West Point and tended to laugh at his shortcomings. "Oh, you know how George is" was their attitude. His shortcomings were less laughable for a soldier under his command.

Gen. Maurice Rose commanded the Third Armored Division. He traveled with his tanks and was killed doing it. Patton traveled in a command car, visited forward positions at times but the idea that Patton "led" his troops in battle is absurd. He led them from a tent to the rear where he made decisions from a map with his dog, Willie, at his feet.

I don't criticize Patton for being behind the lines because it's where the general of an Army should be. I criticize his extensive public relations staff for popularizing the notion that he was a front line general. It was a notion he didn't discourage.

. . .

Patton's daughter, Mrs. James Totten, wrote me a one sentence letter that read simply "Dear Mr. Rooney, My father wouldn't have liked you, either."

Mrs. James W. Totten
So. Hamilton, Massachusetts

Dear Mrs. Totten,

Your letter was one of the best I ever got—short and to the point.

Your father did know me as a *Stars and Stripes* correspondent. We met twice and I can promise you, he didn't like me. "Met" is not quite the word. I had written something he didn't like and he let me know about it when a group of reporters was talking to him. Or he to them.

I liked what you said about your father on the broadcast called "The Generals." I was pleased to know that he was a father who engendered affection and loyalty in his daughter. It makes me think better of him.

. . .

Mrs. Elaine Margarites
Mt. Prospect, Illinois

Dear Mrs. Margarites,

Thank you for your good letter. I was much amused by the copies of "Jane," the British comic strip. During the war, the artist drew very few panels in which Jane didn't find some occasion to take off most of her clothes.

Today "Jane" would be considered almost prudish because she never went beyond bra and panties and her behavior was in modest good taste.

London newspapers were, and still are, poor by our standards but occasionally they have some feature that is different and original and "Jane" was that. It was a great joke widely read and enjoyed by American soldiers.

As for your husband's statement that his outfit had built "the longest pontoon bridge ever built in Europe," most American engineer outfits made some similar claim. After British engineers ran into repeated claims by GI engineers, they finally put a plaque on one of their bridges that read simply "THERE IS NOTHING OUTSTANDING ABOUT THIS BRIDGE."

. . .

Robert R. Denny
Bethesda, Maryland

Dear Bob,

Thanks for sending your remarks at the 306th Bomb Group banquet in Pittsburgh. They were good.

Selling a manuscript like yours is difficult. I don't know whether you'll find a market for this or not. I'm a notoriously poor judge. I'll tell you a story that illustrates my lack of judgment.

Don Bevan, a tail gunner with the 306th Bomb Group, and a former *New York Daily News* cartoonist, used to provide *The Stars and Stripes* with action drawings after he'd been on a raid. I saw him frequently at the air base. Don was shot down and captured.

More than a year later when we overran the prison camp where he was, I met him walking back toward our lines. All he could talk about was not his freedom but a play he and a friend named Ed Tryzinski, had written for his fellow-prisoners called "Stalag 17."

I humored him by accepting a manuscript. After reading it, I had little thought that he'd ever sell it anywhere but I sent it to an agent I'd dealt with in New York. As you know, *Stalag 17* was a hit as a movie and made Don and Ed millions.

A few years later, they successfully sued CBS on the grounds that CBS stole their idea for the series, *Hogan's Heroes*, from them.

So much for my literary judgment.

Bob Denny's book Aces, *was published.*

. . .

When Gen. Curtis LeMay died, I wrote a newspaper column about him that was both laudatory and critical.

John T. Chain, Jr.
General, USAF
Commander in Chief
Strategic Air Command

Dear Gen. Chain,

Your letter revealed your loyalty to Gen. LeMay better than it revealed the kind of logical mind we need in a position as important as the one you hold.

1. I did not say I didn't know Curtis LeMay. I knew him. I knew him first as a colonel with the 306th Bombardment Group at Thurleigh, England, and spoke to him throughout the war and several times thereafter.

2. You tell me LeMay was "a dynamic leader and an integrator of air tactics which helped the allies successfully prosecute the war." I assume you mean "innovator" not "integrator" but whatever you meant, I know it and said so in my column: ". . . he was the kind of guy who won the war for us."

I also said, in a statement that could hardly be considered derogatory, that people would not have learned, from reading his obituary, "how much he did for our Country. He was just the best bomb group commander there ever was." He commanded the 305th at Chelveston.

3. I did not suggest his carrying out the President's order to bomb Japan was wrong. I don't know whether it was wrong or not. LeMay himself was quoted later in his career as saying that we could have won the war without the nuclear bomb, suggesting he thought it was wrong.

4. You tell me "The Marines alone lost 2500 men at Tarawa . . . ". You err in giving me a condescending lecture about World War II. See the chapter on Tarawa in my book *The Fortunes of War: Four Great Battles of WW II.* (Little, Brown, 1966).

5. You tell me, referring to WW II, "It was a tough war." Please, General. I was there.

You tell me about the time-consuming job of training a bomber crew. I was trained and flew with the 8th AF on daylight bombing missions into Germany. (Did you know it was LeMay who realized one waist gunner couldn't man both the inside and outside machine guns and insisted the B17s carry ten-man crews instead of the nine they had been carrying? Probably not.)

6. Your tortuous defense of Gen. LeMay's decision to run on a ticket with George Wallace was comparable to Rommel's defense of his association with Hitler.

7. You state my column on Gen. LeMay "contributes nothing to our society, and only demonstrates a deep bias and cowardice."

You either don't understand or don't agree with the journalist's belief that what serves society best is all the truth about everything.

I resent your remark about cowardice. It was based on no information about my record, war or peace.

I respect your title and share your admiration for Curtis LeMay as a genuine American war hero but I probably know more details of his greatness—and of his shortcomings—than you do.

. . .

Dear Mr. Scanlan,

Thank you for the copy of *The Stars and Stripes* with my article on the raid in the B26. I had totally forgotten the story and the episode and was pleased to be reminded of it. I flew with the B17s, and the B26s were a weekend off by comparison.

I don't know what your experience was—its time frame. I went to an airfield at Bury-St. Edmunds for the first B26 raid. The Air Force held high hopes for the plane as a low-level bomber. Seventeen B26s went out that day to hit the submarine pens at St. Nazaire. The plan was for them to go in so low that the flugzugen abwher canonen, from whence came the word "flak" for the German anti-aircraft weapon, would have no time to zero in on them as they came over the horizon. Incredibly, no one had considered what would happen when the B26s went back out over the channel, exposed to the German guns lining the coast. ETA (Estimated Time of Arrival) passed by a minute, two minutes, ten minutes, an hour. None, not one, of those seventeen B26s got back that day. Every single one shot down with their pilots and six-man crews killed.

Military censors would not allow me to write the story and I had no stomach for doing so anyway.

The whole B26 project was shelved for four to six months before any went out again—this time at 12,000 feet.

Thanks for your offer of a toast. I was toasted several years ago by some of the B17 crews I flew with. The tail gunner who proposed the toast grasped the stem of his glass with just three fingers. He'd lost the others to frostbite. And he was toasting me!

. . .

As a major, Al Smith led the 116th Infantry Regiment onto Omaha Beach, D-Day, June 6, 1944.

Major General Albert H. Smith, Jr.
Tucson, Arizona

Dear Al,

I enjoyed your article in *Army History.*

Next week I'm going to Chicago for a symposium being held by the Naval Institute at Cantigny, the good little 1st Division museum on the grounds of the McCormick estate. You must have been there. There are some good historians coming so I'll be in over my head. I'm listed as luncheon speaker on the subject "COVERING THE INVASION." I'm an imposter, of course.

I've always tried to make it clear I didn't go in on D-Day but it's getting so if you were within a hundred miles of the Normandy beaches on June 6th, you can say you went in on D-Day. There must have been several hundred news people alone there from what I've heard as everyone's memory of where they actually were, fades. You might think there were so many journalists there that we hardly needed you infantrymen.

I came into Utah beach under relatively peaceful circumstances on D-plus–4—and I'm proud of that. I can talk to the historians about covering the war in Normandy as a newspaperman *after* the Invasion and that's what I'll do. I'll leave D-Day to the genuine participants like yourself.

. . .

John C. Fryer, Jr.
Major General, USAF
National War College
Washington, D.C.

Dear General Fryer,

Thank you for your invitation to speak at the National War College's 50th anniversary celebration of the campaign in Northwest Europe.

I am disappointed in having to say I cannot be with you that day.

Perhaps you'll see something else I can do for the War College down the line. Keep me in mind for the 100th Anniversary of D-Day, June 6th, 2044.

PART SIX

English As She Is Writ

John Mitchell
The Daily Express, London

Dear Mitch,

You're missing a lot living over there.

You would have enjoyed the crowd in Bleecks yesterday. It included John Lardner, Red Smith, John Crosby and Dick Maney all playing the match game. Ben Price came in all excited about having just been on a brief demonstration flight of the new Boeing 747 at La Guardia.

Benny said there were several well-known people on board and after they landed, Ben headed for the men's room. He noticed that the man standing next to him at the urinal was Carl Sandburg and he was pretty excited about it.

Benny said "What did you think of the trip, Sir?"

The great American poet looked up at Benny through the thatch of white hair hanging over one eye and said, "That's one hell of an airplane, ain't it?"

So much for the literary elite.

Hope to see you soon, here or there.

Helen Gurley Brown
Editor
Cosmopolitan Magazine

Dear Helen,

You're a friendly person. I wish I could do that.

You'll be pleased to know that you made the deadline for a list I'm keeping of friends who have written during my time of trouble, with days to spare. The original cutoff day was to have been Friday, March 8th. Your letter was postmarked March 6th so there was never any doubt about your eligibility.

I once wrote for *Cosmo* and Joe McCarthy, the editor at the time, gave me the best advice a freelance magazine writer ever got. Joe gave it to me in Toots Shor's when I was trying to make a living at it.

"It isn't hard," Joe said. "Just find out what the editor wants, how long he wants it and get it to him the day he has to have it. It doesn't have to be very good."

Affectionate regards and just plain regards to David.

. . .

Robert Meskil
LOOK Magazine
New York, New York

Dear Mr. Meskil,

Although I hesitate to appear too pleased on the chance there might have been more money in it for me if I'd asked, I was very satisfied with my experience writing the article for *LOOK* and I'd like to try to interest you in something else.

1. THE COMEDY WRITERS might make a good piece. American humor these days is dominated by a handful of people, mostly men, and largely unknown to the public. They are the highest paid writers in the world. I think of Nat Hiken, Coleman Jacoby, Bill Morrow, Nat Perrin, Neil Simon, Lennie Stern, Vinnie Bogert, Goodman Ace, Tony Webster.

How do they write humor? Who says what's funny? Do they have a philosophy about humor? What do they think of the comedians they write for? Are all the comedians funny or just good actors reading their words? Who is easy and who is hard to write for?

2. WHAT HAPPENS TO OLD RACE HORSES? The story of America's horse population might be interesting itself but the fate of old runners has several appealing elements. The best horses live like rich men's kids for the first few years of their lives but breeding has become such a highly organized big business that only a few of the very best horses with great records on the track get to stand at stud and continue living in the manner to which they became accustomed when they were racing, once their career is over.

I'm sure a good editor like you could cut that sentence in half.

Most horses have a natural life of at least twenty years. They race for four. Then what happens to them? It would be done with pictures.

3. When Dan Miche was first looking at the Godfrey piece, he was annoyed when I said *LOOK* didn't have much of a sense of humor.

All I meant was that the magazine doesn't *use* much humor.

I'd like to try some little essays with pictures. Like what? Editors always want to know "like what?"

Well, like WHERE DO WE PUT THINGS?

We put things on top of each other. We hang things over arms of chairs and from doorknobs. Men hang pants from dresser drawers and their change falls out. They hang towels over shower bars and put books on radiators. They put magazines like *LOOK* on the floor next to their chair. They don't put the car in the garage because the garage is full of other things and they don't know where they put the keys to the car.

It would be a slight piece but could be fun.

4. *LOOK* TAILS A PRIVATE EYE. Hire a private investigator and ask him to follow and otherwise find out everything he can about another private investigator, using the methods he uses.

You can see I want work.

. . .

Dear Ms. Worth,

Thank you for your invitation to the poetry reading next Tuesday evening at the YMCA, by what you call "three outstanding local versifiers."

I don't understand most poems when they're printed, even after I've read them over several times. If I don't understand a poem in print, how could I understand a poem that's read aloud just once, and often poorly, by its author?

I don't like to sound like a know-nothing but it is my opinion that most of the people who call themselves poets are no more poets than all the people who paint pictures are artists.

I don't know when poets decided the end of one line doesn't have to rhyme with the end of the next one—or, at the very least, the one after that. To me, if it doesn't rhyme, it isn't poetry. Robert Frost said: "Writing free verse is like playing tennis with the net down."

Carl Sandburg, whose work I often confuse with Robert Frost's, said "poetry is a spot about half way between where you listen and where you wonder what it was you heard."

I still read some poetry in *Harper's*, *The Atlantic* and *The New Yorker* just to make sure I still don't like it. I don't know whether it's my lack of taste or lack of intellect that fails to attract me to modern poetry. I'm careful to say "modern" because there are hundreds of old poems and books of poetry that I like and reread. Most of what I like rhymes. Modern poets feel superior to poets, new and old, whose verses rhyme. They are brothers-in-art to the painters who don't feel that what they put on canvas has to be OF anything. All of it, the paint and the poetry has so much hidden meaning that it hurts my teeth to think of.

Some newspapers print poems regularly. They are often either unintelligible or just plain bad. I'd like to meet an editor who chooses the poetry and ask him a few questions.

"Am I not a person of average intelligence who should be able to comprehend a poem?"

"Why don't I?"

"Am I culturally retarded?"

"Heaven forbid and I hardly dare mention it but . . . are you sure it isn't the poet's fault?"

"Is there any possibility that the poet conned you, the editor, into thinking there was more content to his words than is apparent to me from reading them?"

When I was in high school, I could get all choked up reading Edna St Vincent Millay. In her later years she wrote about getting old.

"I only know that summer sang in me
A little while, that in me sings no more."

Pardon me for saying so, Edna, but now that I'm old it strikes me as pretentious hot air. Life—summer, winter, fall or spring—sings in me as it always did and I don't want the music to stop.

I'll tell you why I think poets write lines whose meaning isn't clear. I think that they don't have a clear idea themselves of what it is they're trying to say. I further think that if they did have a clear idea and wrote it down clearly as prose, it wouldn't amount to much.

Tell me I'm wrong but explain clearly why. Poets themselves have always been defensive about poetry. In college I read Shelley's "A Defence of Poetry." Shelley was a poet I understood and I wonder if he'd defend the modern poets?

Maybe you could make the readings by the three poets more interesting next week to people who don't care much for poetry, by making a contest out of it. Give two prizes—one to the poet who reads best and another to the one whose poems are judged to be best. A crass contest like that might bring the poets back down to earth—where they belong.

. . .

Anyone whose name is known to more than ten people gets frequent requests from people assembling what they call "a celebrity cookbook." Years ago I got one from a columnist for The New York Times, *Enid Nemy, whose work I had read and admired. She said she was putting together a book of favorite potato recipes of well-known people and would like a contribution from me.*

In a moment of pique, I put down an outrageously impractical recipe for "Baked potato ice cream" and sent it to her with a note:

Dear Enid,

When dinner is over and I disappear into the kitchen my guests invariably start chatting incoherently in anxious anticipation of what I've prepared for dessert. (Do I have the genre so far?)

Although I hesitate to select one potato recipe as my best I must say that I get a great many favorable comments on my potato ice cream. Don't serve this to guests who are calorie conscious.

Take four large Idaho potatoes. Peel them, setting the peels aside. Cut the potatoes longwise into half inch slices. Discard the rounded, top and bottom slices. Place the stack of slices, which now have a flat surface, on the cutting board and slice them again, producing long fingers of potato. Turn these parallel to the edge of the cutting board and slice them once more into small cubes.

In six cups of water, to which you have added a cup and a quarter of sugar, simmer the potato cubes until the water evaporates and one of the cubes adheres to a single chopstick. Place cooked potatoes in blender with two cups of heavy cream and a dash of paprika for color and blend until well . . . blended. My mother, who taught me how to make this used to serve it to us as a treat when we were good.

Pour the potato mixture into a divided ice cube tray and place in freezer. If you have a microwave freezer, all the better. When mixture begins to thicken, but before it hardens, insert one toothpick in each cube and continue freezing. Mixture should be of such consistency that the toothpick stands upright. When toothpick no longer pulls out easily or turns blue, the potato ice cream cubes are ready. Plan on three cubes per guest and serve with a bowl of rich chocolate sauce for dipping.

After dinner, throw out the potato peels.

I assumed Enid would smile and throw out the "recipe." Six weeks later I got a call from her editor. "How many will this serve?" she asked. The publisher of Ms. Nemy's book included it in the collection. Ms. Nemy, an otherwise sensible journalist, was furious when she found out or realized that my recipe was a joke. I lost Enid as a friend. She no longer speaks when we pass. So much for parody.

Undaunted, a woman named Susan Parris wrote saying she was assembling her own celebrity cookbook to raise money for her son's school and, having heard of the Baked Potato Ice Cream fiasco, chastised me in a letter. I responded.

Mrs. Susan Connolly Parris
Trenton, New Jersey

Dear Mrs. Parris,

There's a great deal of idiocy about celebrity in America and I have no desire to contribute to it. Enid Nemy is a big girl now and if she undertook to collect a cookbook she should, at the very least, have known enough about food to recognize a joke when she read one.

I don't think any responsible publisher would issue a cookbook without having kitchen-tested the recipes.

There are two possibilities:

1. They tested my recipe for Baked Potato Ice Cream and found it to be delicious.

2. They knew it was a joke and thought it would be fun to have in a book that no one would take seriously anyway.

As for your own celebrity cookbook, making an effort may relieve a helpless feeling you have but I suspect the proceeds will amount to less than a few well-directed requests from rich friends would net for your son's school.

Sorry we disagree. It's my opinion celebrity cookbooks are nonsense and should be treated as such.

I wrote the publisher at Putnam after getting back the corrected proofs to my 1989 book Not That You Asked.

Neil Nyren
Putnam

Dear Neil,

When I put together the manuscript of the collection comprising 129 of my newspaper columns, I put commas where I wanted them. When the columns were originally sent out, an editor at a newspaper or at the Tribune Syndicate often added a comma after an "or" or an "and", where I had not put one. They shouldnt be there. Most of my commas should stay where I put them.

The rules about commas are loose. The fuddy duddy copy editor put a comma in front of every "but" I wrote. There may have been a time when a comma was called for in front of a conjunction like but, but those days are gone forever. I put a comma between those two buts because it would have been confusing without it. That's what commas are for—to eliminate confusion and give a sentence pace.

The greatest grammarian of them all, H.W. Fowler, said a long time ago "anyone who finds himself putting down several commas close to one another should reflect that he is making himself disagreeable."

A lot of people hear the rhythm of my speaking voice when they read what Ive written and I have that in mind when I punctuate. Some of the comma corrections are acceptable to me but Im not willing to go over all of them again to point out which changes I approve of and which I dont so Id like them left the way they were.

Im not confused about who and whom but not many people use whom in conversational English and I like writing as close as is practical to the way I speak. ("'Whom do you like?' said he, for he had been to night school.")

Whom only sounds right to me occasionally when it's the next word after a preposition. I get a lot of letters from retired grammar school English teachers. They agree with your manuscript editor. If you think a majority of the people who buy this book will be retired grammar school English teachers, leave his/her whoms and all your commas in place. Otherwise, Id like them out.

I almost never but not absolutely never, use the obsolescent subjunctive. If this be incorrect, sue me.

My manuscript was consistent with numbers. Ten and under was spelled out. Numbers higher than ten were represented with digits.

This is standard newspaper style but I dont really care if reversing that style is the kind of makework that amuses someone at your place. It's half a dozen of 1 and six of the other.

About dates: "May 7th" reads better than "May 7". Id like several dozen ths put back where I had them after a number.

Even though I know *The Times* and the AP do not, I always capitalize President when it's the President of The United States and Id like it left that way. You notice I capitalize the whole name of the Country, too, including the article which is part of the name. The United States of America. I capitalize Country too when it's "Our Country". That keeps it from being confused with the domain of the farmer. Or Nation when it's our Nation. I know this is arbitrary. When the manuscript editor writes a book, he can put his commas where he likes them and send a copy to the president of the United States. It wont be bush.

(I write my letters without apostrophes denoting an elision in most cases, too. "Dont", "isnt", "arent", "wont." With "I'll", I use one for obvious reasons. I realize this may be impractical for the book and avoided doing it at great inconvenience because such is my habit.)

Otherwise regards,

Andy Rooney

Richard Allen

Dear Dick,

It was good to hear from you even with a complaint about my grammar. I'd probably accept your invitation to speak to one of your classes in the Spring. I can't imagine teaching. I could tell a class everything I know the first couple of days and after that, I'd be faking it.

When you quote R.W. Burchfield's revised version of Fowler's *Modern English Usage* to me as your authority though, you've made a bad choice. I've spent several hours comparing it with the original and Burchfield comes off badly.

I also read Burchfield's complaint about the criticism he got for it. If he didn't expect criticism for rewriting and unimproving Fowler, he should have written his own book with his own name on it. That way, he'd find out whether "Burchfield" would ever become synonymous with proper English usage as Fowler has.

Writing about clichés Fowler's says "any writer who uses the phrase 'If and when' lays himself open to the entirely reasonable suspicion . . . that he likes verbiage for its own sake."

Of the same phrase, Burchfield says "There are circumstances, it seems to me, when the conjoined pair has an independent value . . . "

That sounds like hot air to me and I'm even suspicious of Burchfield's "conjoined pair." Is that different from just a plain pair? What's with "conjoined"?

Fowler wouldn't have liked Burchfield.

The people who write books about grammar and English usage fall in two categories. One group records the way we use the language and usually concludes that use has made it right. The other people stick to their grammatic principles. They tell you what's right without hedging and they insist that's the way it should be no matter how many modern writers can be quoted using it in some other way.

Every time I use a hyphen arbitrarily, I think of Fowler.

He says "the hyphen is not an ornament and should not be placed between two words that do not require uniting and can do their work equally well separate."

Fowler is so opinionated, you can read his reference book like a novel, wondering what's coming up next.

In 1969, when I wrote that show for CBS called "Of Black America" for Bill Cosby, I was uneasy with the word "black." It was new at the time and they had always been called Negroes. "Negro" always seemed like a good, strong, honorable word to me. I thought it was better than "black" but the show was Skee Wolff's idea and he named it but at the time, I didn't like it. He turned out to be right, of course. I didn't see it coming.

I mention that because it reminded me of what Fowler said about the confusion Americans had about the spelling of Mohammed and Mohammedan. Way back in 1926 when he wrote it, Fowler admitted that, even then, the spelling was changing from Mahomet to Mohammed. Then Fowler writes "The trouble with letting the learned gentry bully us out of our traditional "Mahomet" is, no sooner have we tried to be good and learn to say "Mohammed" than they are fired up with a zeal to get us a step or two further on the path of truth which at present seems likely to end in Muhammad."

We're still so afraid of offending any religious or ethnic group that we've changed the spelling a dozen times since, trying to humor Muslims. And now, of course, Jesse Jackson is using "African Americans" instead of "blacks."

I don't think of them as African Americans any more than I think of myself as Irish American. I think of all of us as American. And I think that's what Fowler would think.

. . .

In my pursuit of easy money, I submitted the following report to the story editor at two Hollywood studios.

Dear Mr. Walker,

In 1962, I read a two paragraph story in our local newspaper and set out to learn more of the details. It turned out to be monstrously evil and infinitely complex. Most true stories need a little embellishing before they have enough drama to make a successful movie. This one stands alone.

Sometime in October 1962—the date was not noted because it seemed like a routine matter at the time—the Norwalk, Connecticut police headquarters got a call from Eric Rask, of 11 Highbrooke Road. Mr. Rask complained to the sergeant on duty that over the past months he had been harassed by a strange series of phone calls.

On the day previous to his call to the police, Rask's regular oil man had come and filled his tank from a pipe in the lawn that let to the basement. Twice on the morning of the day he first called the police, oil trucks from other fuel companies in the area had driven up and started to fill his already brimming tank. One trucker inserted the nozzle, started the flow of oil from his truck and then, as he regularly did when making his first stop at a house, headed for the basement to check the capacity of the tank and its state of emptiness. By the time he had noted the tank was already full and had bolted back up the cellar stairs for the truck, the fuel oil was flowing over Eric Rask's lawn.

Rask reported that he checked with the oil companies and found that in both cases the caller who ordered the oil deliveries had given the name "Millicent." The Norwalk police, only mildly interested in what seemed like a routine prank, agreed to see what they could find out.

In the next few months Eric Rask and his wife Nedla, were subjected to a barrage of what at first seemed like practical jokes. Dozens of business firms in Norwalk, Westport, Darien, Stamford, and Bridgeport got orders for deliveries to the Rask home. They were all ordered by a feminine voice identified only as "Millicent." If any further identification was asked, the full name was given as "Millicent Rask."

Two local funeral homes delivered caskets to 11 Highbrooke Road. An aunt had died, "Millicent" explained in ordering them.

On six successive days, expensive color television sets were brought to the Rask home.

On several occasions Eric Rask stepped into his car and found it inoperable. A local garage had been given the exact location of the car and had been asked to come up and remove the battery for recharging. They had done so.

The Rasks attended a football game one Saturday and returned to find their gravel driveway stacked high from their garage door to the street with 200 8" x 12" cinder blocks delivered by Hain Brothers Cinder Block Company on the telephoned order of "Millicent."

Columbia and John Cutrone, owners of the Midtown Restaurant in Norwalk, had received an order on Wednesday one week to prepare an elaborate dinner party for twelve to be served at six o'clock sharp the following Friday evening. The order was for nine steak and three lobster dinners—the lobster order, presumably to take care of the Catholic members of the party, gave the call the ring of truth. There were to be three bottles of good vintage champagne, chilled. At 5:50 that Friday night "Millicent" once again called the Midtown. Columbia Cutrone was told that the Rask party was on its way and the steaks and lobsters should be put on the fire.

No one came for the feast and when the Cutrones called Eric Rask, he, of course, knew nothing about it.

These orders, as well as the direct calls to the Rask house continued at the rate of three or four a week. In each case when Nedla Rask answered there was no voice on the phone, only unusually heavy breathing.

When a call was made to the Rask home, often from a phone booth, the receiver was left off the hook after the call. This practice left the Rask phone dead until the receiver at the other end was put back on the hook. It made it impossible for the Rasks to call the police or the phone company immediately. On one occasion after a call, Eric Rask rushed from his house to use a neighbor's phone.

He started across the street for the Gamble house and met Jackie Gamble in the middle of the street.

"I just had a call from 'Millicent' " Jackie said.

"My phone's off the hook and I was coming over to use yours."

All the incidents were reported to the police and the police attitude gradually changed from one of indifference to irritation. Several men were assigned to the job on a part-time basis, but it got precedence over nothing and little progress was made in identifying "Millicent."

Highbrooke Road is one block long. It runs between East Avenue and Dry Hill Road. There are sixteen houses on the street and a hill that breaks abruptly one third the way up the street makes it impossible for those at one end to see the houses at the other. Residents of the six houses nearest the brow of the hill can look to either end.

At the end of a year of harassment, Eric Rask, a likeable and normally mild-mannered engineer of thirty-five, was raging mad and wildly frustrated. His wife, Nedla, an attractive brunette who had always enjoyed the day-to-day suburban chores of a mother with two children and an active social life, was close to a nervous breakdown. It was not so much that the practical jokes were not funny but they had about them a strange and diabolical unhealthiness of a very clever abnormal mind.

Nedla Rask, on the advice of her husband, decided to leave home for a three-week rest. She told no one but her immediate family where she was going or, as a matter of fact, that she was going at all. She left in darkness and spent the time at an upstate New York farm owned by her cousin. During this period there were no "Millicent" calls.

Half an hour after Nedla Rask walked into her home after the secret vacation, there was a knock at the front door. The messenger had a large box. Nedla Rask accepted the box, put it on the dining room table, cut the string, folded back the cardboard cover. It was a huge three-layer cake elaborately decorated with the inscription "WELCOME HOME—MILLICENT."

Minutes later the phone rang. The only sound as she listened was that of slightly irregular heavy breathing.

By this time the young and able Town Prosecutor, Abner Sibal had been called into the case. Together with Frank Virgulak, a competent plainclothes detective with the Norwalk force, he made the first effort to organize the campaign to trap "Millicent."

As the details of the case were collected and sorted out, a few facts became apparent.

1. The perpetrator, "Millicent," probably lived within sight of the Rask house. Number 11 could be seen from eight of the houses of

Highbrooke Road and probably clearly enough, through backyards, from three of the houses on East Avenue.

2. Most of the calls were made from phone booths between Bridgeport and Norwalk, many of them from the Westport area.

3. More calls were made Sunday before noon than at any other time.

4. "Millicent's" work seemed to be directed primarily at Nedla Rask.

5. Six changes in the Rask phone number did not halt the calls for more than forty-eight hours, indicating someone had unusual access to either their number indicated on the instrument or phone company records.

6. The case, though minor in some respects, was becoming a major source of embarrassment to the Norwalk police department.

In the light of the facts, half a dozen suspects were singled out. Each had the opportunity and the motive.

Suspect A: Fred and Millie Bunce. The Bunce's lived on East Avenue with a clear view of the rear of the Rask home. Millie had been the chief telephone operator for the city of Norwalk. Her husband, Fred, worked as an engineer for the Southern Bell Telephone Company installing highly specialized telephone equipment. Their knowledge of telephones, access to new numbers and proximity to the Rask house put them high on the list of people to be watched.

Motive: Many of the residents in the neighborhood belonged to the fashionable Shoreham County Club. The Bunce's had applied for membership and had been rejected. There was some talk that the Rasks had voted against them.

Suspect B: Jeremiah Dorney, 16 Highbrooke Road. Mr. Dorney was retired, free most of the day and often spent time on small errands in the area from which the calls came.

Until 1949, Dorney had been chief of police for the city of Norwalk. When a Socialist mayor was elected, he was ousted from office accompanied by a great deal of bickering and unpleasantness.

Motive: Several police officers and politicians considered Mr. Dorney the principal suspect. The actions of "Millicent," they felt, were not directed against the Rasks, but were being done to embarrass the police force. Dorney had good reason to wish for this.

Suspect C: Bob and Fran X. Fran X had been a rape victim in 1954. The crime took place in the X's car with their small child a witness. The X's lived within view of the Rask house.

Motive: Fran X had suffered severe emotional shock and she had never forgotten her nightmarish experience. Many of the neighbors, in private talks with Sibal and Virgulak, felt that Fran X was the most likely "Millicent." They felt her mental condition was such that she was seeking to give the popular and attractive Nedla Rask, a taste of the unhappiness she had experienced. They felt she resented Nedla's friendly, outgoing personality.

Suspect D: Vincent J. (Jackie) Gamble, 12 Highbrooke Road. Jackie Gamble, thirty-eight, lived with his mother and father. He was a successful beer salesman and well-known around Norwalk where he had lived all his life. The Gamble house was directly across from the Rask's and provided the best view of it. Jackie moved around freely and had ample opportunity to make pay station calls.

Motive: A possible motive for Jackie Gamble was not as obvious as some of the others. Some neighbors felt that he was a "Momma's Boy" and that he resented the attention Mrs. Rask offered his mother. On several occasions the Rasks invited Mrs. Gamble to dinner without including Jackie.

Ab Sibal, leaned to the theory that Gamble had a not-quite-normal crush on Mrs. Rask, which manifested itself in these strange intrusions on the private life of the Rasks as a happily married couple.

Suspect E: Eric Rask. The police were constantly getting confidential calls from neighbors and from friends of the Rasks who did not live in the Highbrooke Road area with bits of information pointing clearly to one or another of the prime suspects. On several occasions the callers insisted emphatically that Eric Rask himself was making the "Millicent" calls.

Motive: Informers in the neighborhood claimed Rask had "another woman." Rask's motive, if indeed he was "Millicent," was to drive his wife out of her mind. Whether it was Rask or not, this was close to being accomplished.

In addition to these five there were other, lesser suspects. One man was trailed by the police for two weeks. His actions were clearly suspicious and he proved to be less than the hard-working homebody that his wife thought he was, but on close questioning police eventually became satisfied that while he was quite a man with several married women around town, he had no hand in the "Millicent" matter.

Mrs. Richard Walkden of 6 Highbrooke Road was a lukewarm prospect as "Millicent" because she had full view of the Rask house and was an accomplished actress who had successfully played a wide variety of parts with the local theater group. It was thought she might be able to give her voice the unusual quality the voice of "Millicent" possessed.

A few of the neighbors even suspected Nedla Rask herself. Although this seemed physically impossible to the investigators, they did not completely rule out the possibility that Nedla had perpetrated the whole affair in some unnatural desire to call attention to herself.

As police surveillance became more intense, "Millicent" became more active. During the first months of the investigation the Rasks had been the only victims but as the case entered its second year "Millicent's" operation broadened in scope, to include neighbors and friends.

On September 9th, 1963, a coal truck drew up in front of the carefully kept oil-heated home of John Wallace. The men on the truck had specific instructions to shove open the window leading to the basement in the right front corner of the house, nearest the driveway. The men opened the window, shoved in their coal chute and opened the trap that allowed five tons of coal to thunder down into the pine-paneled bar and playroom of the Wallace home.

Flowers came to the Walkden's and more oil deliveries for everyone. The Rasks continued to get most attention however.

Men in the neighborhood were up in arms. They were impatient with the police and ready to lynch "Millicent." Nine of them quietly formed a vigilante committee and organized a schedule according to which they were to take turns keeping an eye on the Rask house.

On October 22nd, the vigilante committee met clandestinely in the basement of George E. Cramer's house at Number 17. They had crept in quietly at ten minute intervals in order not to attract attention. No light emanated from the heavily curtained cellar windows.

The meeting had been in progress for less than half an hour when a heavily laden delivery man from a Norwalk catering firm appeared at the door upstairs with beer and sandwiches for everyone. It was an order no one present admitted placing. The vigilante committee dissolved in a solution of mutual suspicion.

During the course of the investigation many friendships had been both made and broken. Abner Sibal, the prosecutor, found the Rasks to be especially pleasant people and on several occasions during the case he and his wife saw them socially. During one dinner party attended by the Rasks, the Sibals and several other friends (some of whom were suspects in the eyes of Sibal and Detective Virgulak), the conversation kept coming back to the "Millicent" episodes. Most of them agreed they were tired of talking about it but could not keep their minds off it. They would agree to forget it and the conversation would flow into other channels. After a brief period someone would make another reference to it and the chatter of informed and uniformed opinion concerning "Millicent's" identity would break out again.

At exactly midnight the party had temporarily side-tracked the topic when the phone rang. There was dead silence and not a doubt in any mind as to who the caller would be.

Sibal asked Mrs. Rask to answer, although the party was not in her house. He listened long enough to hear "Millicent's" deep breathing at the sound of Nedla Rask's voice, then dashed from the house and roared off in the direction of the Post Road where the phone booths most often used late at night by "Millicent" were situated.

Sibal dashed from one booth to another, looking quickly and racing on. At the fifth booth he opened the door and saw the instrument dangling toward the floor.

"Hello?"

"Ab!" It was Nedla Rask on the other end. "Millicent" had fled. Ab Sibal thought he was safe, at least, in eliminating anyone at the party.

During her ordeal, Mrs. Rask was consoled on every hand. Mrs. Walkden often visited her in the morning. Fran X came in often. Everyone tried to help and put themselves out by being nice to the Rasks. Jackie Gamble, across the street, saw to it that they got all the beer they wanted from his employer at rock bottom, wholesale prices. He often went to the Rask house to talk over his own problems with Nedla.

One morning he came in about ten o'clock and after speaking briefly about new episodes in the "Millicent" matter, he asked Nedla if she would read a letter he had received from a woman he was in love with at his office. Nedla declined but Jackie was insistent. He had a terrific problem and he wanted Nedla to read the letter and advise him. After ten minutes urging she consented.

The letter was surprisingly innocuous. The writer professed affection for Jackie, suggested that they had seen each other frequently, although not intimately, and Nedla inferred that the writer was a married woman. Jackie Gamble admitted she was and asked Nedla Rask what she thought he should do. Her advice was mostly evasive.

Less than a week later, Jackie Gamble came to the Rask house with a large box. Inside the house he unwrapped it and revealed an expensive fur cape. He had, he said, bought it as a Christmas present for his girlfriend. It was not yet October but he had been able to get such a good buy, he told Nedla, that he wished she would keep if for him until Christmas so that no one would see it. He was insistent, too, that she not only keep it for him, but wear it. She, of course, refused.

While in retrospect it would seem apparent that Jackie Gamble was actually "Millicent," it was not so obvious at the time. The Rasks were naive in many ways and often it did not occur to them to report significant incidents to Sibal or Detective Virgulak. And in many ways Jackie had seemed like a good friend to the Rasks. At Christmas for several years he had showered the two small Rask children with presents. He gave Ricky, the twelve-year old boy, an expensive wrist watch and his neighborliness seemed genuine.

The facts of the case were obscured by bitterness among the residents on Highbrooke Road; often the bitterness led to false suspicions and exaggerated reports, false tips and off-track clues. For one thing, by this time many of the false deliveries were being made to Jackie Gamble himself. Everyone knew he was a beer salesman and a favorite trick of "Millicent" was to call one of the soft drink distributors in the area and have a dozen cases of Coca Cola left at the Gamble home.

And several of the other suspects could not be dismissed altogether, despite the growing feeling held by Sibal and Virgulak, the two most concerned with the case, that Gamble was actually "Millicent." There was no proof and several incidents that seemed hard to reconcile with the possibility of his guilt, but little bits of evidence kept piling up against Jackie Gamble.

Detective Francis Virgulak, like Gamble, had grown up in Norwalk and things he knew about Gamble began coming back to him. When he was seventeen, Jackie Gamble got the job as head usher at the Empress Theater. The Empress always had a vaudeville show weekends and one of the reasons Jackie liked the job as head usher was because he could see the acts over and over again. Once they had a ventriloquist on stage and this fascinated Jackie most of all. When the act left the Empress, he found an ad in the back of a magazine promising to teach anyone the art of "throwing the voice." Jackie took the mail-order course and became proficient as an amateur ventriloquist.

Virgulak recalls that several times in the mid 1930s when he was passing the Empress Theater, he'd hear a mocking feminine voice that appeared to be coming from an upstairs window, call softly "Hello Francis." He remembered the smiling face of Jackie Gamble standing innocently nearby.

If Jackie Gamble was "Millicent," what was his motive and how could it be proved? Although Nedla Rask had steadfastly sworn that Jackie Gamble's behavior with her had never been other than gentlemanly, Sibal thought that Gamble had what he called a "crush" on Mrs. Rask. He used the word "crush" to describe an attitude that was not quite adult. Sibal and the police pursued this and while they did not neglect other suspects, they continued to consider Gamble the most probable.

Jackie belonged to several clubs and played cards frequently at one of them with a regular group. Police talked with everyone who knew

Gamble; he had few real friends. From one they got a report that fitted the strange reports of the heavy breathing which so often greeted Nedla Rask when she answered the phone. Gamble's crony testified to police that on one occasion he entered the Gamble house unexpectedly and it was his belief that Jackie was simultaneously telephoning and masturbating.

A three-car tail was put on Jackie Gamble whenever he left the house. Three unmarked police cars leap-frogged their positions behind his new Oldsmobile so that, looking in the back mirror, he would not see the same car behind him after every turn. His Sunday morning pattern was the same. He took his mother to Mass, drove around rather aimlessly and returned home about noon.

During the week he made sales calls regularly at large grocery stores between Bridgeport and Stamford, stopping often at a few favorite hangouts in between. One of them was a tavern directly across from the State police barracks in Westport, which seemed to provide an answer to one of the minor mysteries in the case—the origin of the pseudonym "Millicent." Gamble left the tavern after a visit one day, and a detective went in, partly to see if the phone was off the hook in the booth, and partly to ask a few questions about Gamble's habits.

The detective ordered a beer, looked around and his eyes fell on the license required to be displayed over all bars in Connecticut. It read "PERMITTEE: MILLICENT L. BOWE."

The major problem, if Gamble was in fact "Millicent," which seemed highly probable now, was to lay a trap for him that would provide evidence that would stand up in court. Many of the things that had been done were unsettling, highly irritating and maddeningly clever—but they were not serious crimes. Not only was there no law protecting a citizen from this sort of devilment, but proof was extremely hard to get.

The police will not say specifically how "Millicent" was trapped, but it is apparent that it involved an arrangement with the telephone company which The Telephone Company would rather not talk about either. It can be assumed that all calls going into the Rask house were not only monitored, but traced immediately. It is quite possible that the Gamble house phone was also tapped, an action that neither police nor phone company officials admit or used in court.

The Norwalk police were reluctant to admit they could not catch "Millicent." There is always considerable rivalry between local and state police bodies and although Chief Max Orlins of Norwalk was reluctant to do it, the Westport Barracks "G" of the Connecticut State Police was finally called in. The action was taken chiefly because certain incidents occurred outside Norwalk's boundaries. Many of the calls had come from beyond city limits and perhaps fifty of the false orders had been placed with oil companies, funeral homes and stores in towns from Bridgeport to Stamford, a distance of forty miles.

On February 6th, 1964, a Sunday, the trap was carefully laid. Abner Sibal and Detective Frank Virgulak were at Police Headquarters in Norwalk and every available police car was on alert and cruising near the areas from which the calls were most often made.

At about 10:30 a call was received in the Westport Barracks by Officer Keller. As soon as the caller identified himself as "Eric Rask," Keller gave the signal to another police officer to have the call traced. By coincidence, Norwalk Police Chief Orlins was at the State Police Headquarters at the time conferring in another room with a lieutenant about the "Millicent" case. He was informed of the call and immediately contacted Virgulak and Sibal in the Norwalk office.

"Eric Rask" told Keller, as this was happening, that he was calling from a phone booth at a gas station on the Merritt Parkway near Exit 38. He reported that his car had just been struck by a hit-and-run driver. He further reported that while he was not seriously injured, his car was damaged and he had been able to get the license number of the car that had hit him. It was a blue Chevrolet station wagon Connecticut license RHFH. He said that if they had to reach him to call Victor 7–4236.

Keller was able to engage "Rask" in conversation, pressing for details for almost four minutes. The call had been traced immediately and located as originating from a pay phone in a small news and stationery on East Avenue in Norwalk. This information was given to Sibal and Virgulak at Norwalk headquarters and a patrol car with Pat Rooney and Charlie Wagner was dispatched by radio.

Wagner and Rooney pulled up in front of Lewis's Stationery Store in time to see Jackie Gamble walk out the door. They did not stop him but waited until he had left and then entered the store themselves. The proprietor knew Gamble. He said that he had just used the telephone and been in the store in the last five minutes.

The police waited about an hour and then called the number the person reporting the hit-and-run accident had given. Jackie Gamble answered. Officer Keller announced himself and asked if he was speaking to Eric Rask. Jackie Gamble showed surprise, said he was not; that Mr. Rask lived across the street. Gamble said that he did not think Mr. Rask had been involved in an accident because he had seen him home within the last hour. Gamble said "Millicent" had probably given the Police his number as a further harassment. The police knew the call had come, not from Eric Rask, but from "Millicent"; they also knew the reason Jackie Gamble's phone number had been given was a devious one. Three months ago it might have thrown them off the track.

(Several months previous to this police had been puzzled by a call from "Millicent" that came as friends were gathered in the living room of the Gamble home on the occasion of a wake being held for Jackie's father. At that time the phone rang everyone heard it. Jackie answered the phone and carried on a conversation, of which the guests could only hear his end, purportedly with "Millicent." It later became apparent that Jackie had dialed "9494," a Norwalk code that rings the phone from which the number was dialed after the receiver is put back in the cradle.)

By luck, this first time the caller "Millicent" had been almost positively identified leaving the scene of the phone call at the stationery store, was also the first time the call involved an actual law violation. Falsely reporting an accident is a misdemeanor comparable to turning in a false fire alarm.

Monday morning the police called Gamble again and asked him to come to the State Police Barracks in Westport. They hoped to face him with the evidence and get a confession from him. When the police hung up, Gamble immediately crossed the street to the Rask house. Had the police seen him head for Nedla Rask they might reasonably have been worried for her safety.

Friendly and polite as ever, Gamble told Nedla that the police wanted him for questioning and asked if she would go to Westport with him. By this time Nedla had been informed of police suspicions that Jackie Gamble was actually "Millicent."

She was naturally panic-stricken, but she quickly agreed to go with Gamble if he would give her a few minutes to get ready. It was agreed he would pick her up in ten minutes. He left the house and Nedla called the police. Sibal, the prosecutor, and Virgulak were most concerned with her safety on hearing this. They told her the best thing would be to go with Gamble and that they would make certain she was protected with trailing police cars.

The trip was without incident and Gamble pulled into the State Police Barracks a short time later armed with a magnificent air of innocence. On being questioned, he said that he knew nothing about the false report on the hit-and-run accident on the Merritt Parkway. He admitted having been in Lewis's Stationery Store, but said that he had called his girl in Rye from there. After two years evading the whole Norwalk Police Department, Gamble was trapped. 1. The phone booth had been checked and no long distance calls had been made from it on Sunday, February 6th. Rye was long distance. 2. Officer Keller had been careful not to mention the location of the fictitious hit-and-run accident. When Gamble gave its location as "the Merritt Parkway" this was a fact only the person who made the call would have known.

Jackie Gamble was defended in Norwalk City Court by Alfred Santaniello and prosecuted by Abner Sibal. After hearing a long string of witnesses, Judge Virginia Boyd found him guilty of falsely reporting an accident and sentenced him to thirty days with $30 fine.

The case was appealed before Judge Milton H. Meyers in the Common Pleas Court in Bridgeport. This time Gamble was found guilty on the same charge, fined $50 with thirty days in jail, two years probation with sentence suspended on the condition Gamble accepted psychiatric advice.

The case was closed but the wounds, laid open and rubbed with salt for two years on Highbrooke Road, have healed, but slowly. Most of those involved have found it easiest to move away; Eric Rask quit his job and moved away.

This story is still for sale cheap to any motion picture producer who can use it.

Elizabeth Peale Allen
PLUS Magazine
Pawling, New York

Dear Mrs. Allen,

Thank you for your invitation to write my Great Moment in Positive Thinking for *PLUS Magazine*. As a person who tried to make a living as a freelance magazine writer for several years, my pulse still quickens when I get a letter from an editor.

While I was an admirer of your father, Norman Vincent Peale, I'm afraid that anything I'd have to say about religion would not be what you're looking for. I recall one Great Moment in Positive Thinking when I was about twelve. My mother had sent me to Sunday School at the Madison Ave. Presbyterian Church in Albany but I had several Catholic friends I played with.

One day I got into an argument with one of them, Alfie Gordon, over the question of the virgin birth. I came home and told my mother Alfie's story about what a ghost had done to Mary.

"Presbyterians believe that, too, Andrew" she told me.

My great moment in thinking that day was that I was positive I wasn't a Catholic or a Presbyterian and I never went to church again.

Thank you for asking me but I think you can see, I'm not the person for the job.

D. Anthony English
Executive Editor
MacMillan Publishing Co.

Dear Mr. English,

I'm amused to note that publishers now have executive editors and you're one. We've had executive producers in television for years. They are often the producers who don't really produce anything.

Speed reading is nothing that ever interested me and after ignoring or just not getting at Royce Adams's letters asking for permission to use an article I wrote in his speed reading exercise book, I finally did write and tell him I didn't want my piece used.

Like most writers, I wish people would spend *more* time reading my work, not less. It doesn't seem right for me to be a party to teaching something I don't approve of.

I am, however, not inclined to be litigious and if my article is already in the book I will probably put off suing for years. I sue as slow as I read.

. . .

Erica Hatridge
Kirkwood, Missouri

You should get mad more often when you're writing. I liked your second letter a lot.

I'm always impressed with anyone who likes and is good at, mathematics. It's a strange confession for a writer to make but progress in our world depends on the hard sciences, like mathematics, more than on the kind of thing I do. Without science, the quality of our culture and the arts would certainly decline. I'm not sure the reverse is true.

If I were a teacher writing margin notes on your letter I'd stop at your second word. "When one is a . . . " The word "one," used as a third person substitute for a first person pronoun in an attempt to be modest, is awkward and stilted. It sounds particularly artificial coming from a thirteen-year old girl. It's nothing serious but I'd avoid using it if I were you.

The word "alas," beginning your third sentence, is old-fashioned and I'd recommend avoiding that, too. It's from the Latin "lassus" meaning weary and it's a good word with bad vibes. Maybe Shakespeare ruined it for the rest of us with "Alas, poor Yorick!"

You end your letter by asking me to tell you about myself. I'm a writer, Erika. It's foolish, rude and presumptuous of you to expect me to write to one young woman in Kirkwood, Missouri, and give her my life story.

Thanks for your good letter. We'd be friends.

. . .

Dear Ian,

Thank you for your good letter about typewriters.

Each of my Underwoods has a personality of its own. Even when two look identical and were made the same year they have different traits. The Underwood #5 model was made between 1917 and 1921. They are almost indestructible, although from what you tell me, your wife, Gertrude, would have done better to have submerged yours in gasoline instead of putting it in the bathtub filled with soapy water to clean it.

Writers are always looking for ways to avoid getting to work, and picking dry ink out of the small parts of the a, e and o of my Underwood, with a paperclip, has provided me with a great deal of non-writing hours over the years.

I write mostly on a computer now but I often use the typewriter for letters because I've never mastered doing envelopes on the printer connected to my computer.

. . .

It has always seemed to me that it's best to be frank with kids as long as you make it clear that you like them.

Dear Fifth Graders,

Thank you for all your letters.

I have never thought it was a good idea to talk to children as if they were children. I like to talk to them as if they were people and that's the way I'm going to talk to you in this letter about your letters.

The things you wrote made me sorry that I picked on the fifth grade as my example of students who have not yet had enough experience in life to write anything original. It could have been the third grade or the eighth grade or any other grade. I don't take it back though and nothing any of you said in your letters convinced me that I was wrong. Your letters were not very good because none of you had an idea of your own.

Many of you said the same things. That suggested to me that Mrs. Hegedus gave you the things she thought you might tell me. Many of you said I was wrong in thinking you don't know anything because you said you have memorized the Declaration of Independence. Memorizing what someone else has written is not usually a good way to spend your time and it doesn't have anything to do with the kind of knowledge a writer must have.

I didn't like the colored decorations you put on your letters either. I thought it made them look like kindergarten work. If you have something to say in a letter, you shouldn't have to attract attention to the words by decorating them with hearts and flowers.

Am I being too hard on you? I think you can take it. I like you and I liked getting your letters. I think you're lucky to have a teacher as interested in you as Mrs. Hegedus is. I'm sorry I didn't get to your assembly. The big brown envelope all your letters came in was postmarked May 25th and several of you said your program was to be "Friday May 26th." There was no "Friday May 26th" this year but even if you meant Friday May 29th, it was too late for me to arrange to be there.

One more thing I want to say. You told me you wrote to President Reagan but haven't had an answer yet. Do you know how many fifth grade classes there are in The United States? Do you know how many children there are in each class? How's your arithmetic? Do the multiplication. How many letters would the President get if all the fourth, fifth, and sixth grade classes wrote him letters? Would he also get any letters from the 43 million people who voted for him? From several thousand of his old friends from Hollywood? Writing a letter to the President is about as good a way to spend your time as memorizing Patrick Henry. Writing to people your age in Norwalk, Ohio, and Norwalk, Connecticut, is a good idea. Try to tell them what *you* have observed about living and what you think about school or bicycles or teachers or sidewalks or anything else you really know something about.

. . .

Ed Otte
Greeley Tribune
Greeley, Colorado

Dear Mr. Otte,

I was disappointed to get the note from the Tribune Syndicate that you are dropping my column but I was pleased that you bothered to say my column and Mike Royko's which you are also dropping, had been strong features.

At its peak, the column appeared in 327 papers. I must be down around 250 now and it's hard not to take the decline personally. In my depressed moments I get thinking it isn't good enough or it wouldn't be dropped, no matter what the economic conditions are.

I'm going to have a hard time not hoping your circulation drops off without us.

. . .

Lois DeBakey is the sister of the famous heart surgeon, Michael DeBakey, but she's better known to me than he is because of her work with the English language. For years she has led a crusade, trying to get the medical profession to use plain English instead of technical jargon.

Lois DeBakey
Baylor College of Medicine
Houston, Texas

Dear Lois,

I agree that it was stupid for that doctor to use so many calculated vulgarities as she did talking to Lesley Stahl Sunday night. It was wrong because it lessened her impact and authority.

I'm ambivalent about the use of obscenity in motion pictures, newspapers and on television. Generally I dislike it but there are occasions when it seems appropriate.

In the movie *JFK* there was one particular scene in which the character repeatedly spit forth the vilest kind of language and I thought it served a dramatic purpose. If so many other characters in the picture had not used so much of the same filth in other scenes, it would have served it better.

I've been to a hundred witless Broadway plays in which the actors' only hope for laughs were in the vulgarities they pronounced from time to time in desperation. For some strange reason foul language invariably evokes laughter from an audience.

There's no question the obscenity barriers are all but down. I'm still appalled by the language people use in mixed company in public places. You sit next to someone in a restaurant and the vulgarities and obscenities you can't avoid hearing intrude on your relationship with the person you're sitting with.

President Bush made "screw" acceptable when he used the word in a speech on national television. I had always avoided the phrase in writing or conversation but I do think the phrase "He really got screwed" has a nuance of meaning that transcends the vulgarity of its original sense and is useful. For that reason, a case can be made for its use.

I take a lot of grammatical license with the language for a variety of reasons, one of them being ignorance. Today I was writing about politicians.

"It takes someone with an awful lot of ego to think he's smart enough to be President of the United States . . ." I wrote.

"An awful lot . . . "? "He's smart enough . . . "? What kind of English is that? And shouldn't I have said "to think *he or she* is smart enough . . . "?

I'm not going to rewrite it and make it "he or she," I decided. Too clumsy. I'll take the chance of irritating some women.

But then further along in the piece I wrote "A politician can also simply admit he or she was wrong and apologize." Not consistent with above, I thought to myself, but I'll do it anyway. It doesn't get in the way so much there, I decided.

Most people, in similar circumstances, use "they" even when they started with the singular pronoun, just to avoid the he-or-she dilemma.

When I started as a reporter for *The Stars and Stripes*, I remember facing the question of whether or not to touch up the grammar of a semi-literate soldier I had interviewed and was quoting. I usually did but it depends on the situation. If an illiterate sound to an interview is part of the story, it should be left the way the person said it. Otherwise, you fix it. Very few people speak the language the way they'd prefer to be quoted using it.

It's difficult to strike the right balance between hide-bound and know-nothing in usage when you write the English language.

Broadcast standards are deteriorating so quickly that it's difficult to keep up with what they're down to. For many years CBS News had a great grammarian, Cabel Greet, a Columbia professor, on retainer. We could all turn to him at any time for help and advice on matters of usage or pronunciation but he's long gone.

You are doing noble work. Keep at it.

. . .

Mike Wallace (University of Michigan, '39)
60 Minutes

Dear Mr. Wallace:

In your comment about Jesse Jackson, you referred to "the Reverend Jackson."

There are some basic things about the word "reverend" that even someone with a University of Michigan education should know. First among these is the fact that reverend is an adjective.

Webster's Dictionary of English Usage:

"The word should be preceded by *the*; it should be followed by a surname or a title such as Dr. or Mr.; it is wrong to address a clergyman, as President Reagan did in 1981, as "Reverend Moomaw."

The Chicago Manual of Style:

Refer to "the Reverend George Smith, Father Smith, Mr. Smith or the Reverend Mr. Smith *not* Reverend Smith."

Fowler's Modern English Usage (Under Illiteracies):

"There is a kind of offense against the literary idiom that is not easily named. (examples) Rev. Smith."

A Dictionary of Contemporary American Usage, Bergen Evans:

"To use the title Reverend without a proper name is generally considered undignified."

Modern American Usage, Wilson Follett:

"Neglecting certain usages is a solecism. The chief of these is the article *the* and a first name (or a Mr. or Dr.) with Reverend. A moment's reflection shows why good form makes this demand. The meaning of *reverend* is still active in the title, thanks to the preceding *the,* and the respect it implies calls for the full designation of the man; it is not Blake or *some* Blake or other who is reverend, but Daniel Blake or Mr. Blake. Thus The Reverend Mr. Blake."

Yr obdt svt

Andrew A. Rooney (Colgate '42)

. . .

Marcia Reeves
The Highland Institute

Dear Ms. Reeves,

I have the memo asking for my support for your writing "workshop" and would like to point out something you seem to already know: Inflating prose is an art all by itself and might be a course you should teach.

How about a Hot Air Workshop? It would offer a one-week PhD to any student who could take a simple idea and, in five days, blow it up with words that made it unrecognizable.

From the brochures you included, I think it must be one of your school's principal areas of expertise. You would make it clear to the kids that ordinary words don't do it if they're trying to make an idea sound more important than it is.

Just a few examples, which I'm reminded of by your letter:

Always use "Workshop" for "Class." ("Session" or "Study Group" are possible alternatives.)

Refer to a person's "Skills" when you mean "skill."

Call any teacher you have a "Mentor," not a plain old, ordinary teacher.

"Young minds" would always be preferable to "kids." And your group would, of course, not be just teaching, you'd be "shaping" those "young minds."

Other than that, I support what you are doing but I will be unable to join you there this summer.

. . .

Neil Nyren
Putnam

Dear Neil,

Thanks for sending along *Leaving Home*, the new Art Buchwald book. Mike Wallace says it's interesting—not that Mike's much of a literary critic and he and Buchwald are unlikely best friends. He calls him "Artie."

It may seem unlikely too but I'm enthusiastic about Buchwald. I'd even go so far as to say I think he's underrated as an American humorist.

As for the jacket blurb you want, I don't do them but how would this be?

"ART BUCHWALD AND I HAVE AN AGREEMENT. HE DOESN'T READ MY BOOKS AND I DON'T READ HIS. I'VE HEARD THIS ONE IS VERY GOOD. ANDY ROONEY."

Thanks for the report on *Sweet and Sour*. The sales are sort of a mystery, aren't they? The first two books sold almost a million copies each. People keep saying to me "I read your book." I always say "Books." No one realizes there have been eight now.

I think they all look the same and once someone bought one of them, they figured they had all the Andy Rooney they wanted. It was probably a mistake to put my picture on the cover of every one of them. It made all of them look more like the same book.

But I'm not complaining. The sales aren't that bad.

. . .

I do not have many heroes but the great essayist, E.B. White, was one. He put down the English language simply and directly better than anyone else I ever read. I was pleased that I got to know him well enough in the process of making a film from his 10,000 word gem, Here Is New York, *to be comfortable calling him by his nickname, "Andy."*

E.B. White
North Brooklin, Maine

Dear Andy,

It has given me a lot of class among my friends to have been mentioned, albeit as a footnote, in your book.

It comes to my mind once or twice a week that you should be talked into submitting to a long interview or conversation, on film. Would you say no if I asked? I ask.

The process wouldn't be painless but neither should it be excruciating for you. We would sit and talk for an hour or two on successive days before a camera. I'd try to get you to say things about almost anything . . . writing, farming, God, tools, friends, food, patriotism. Anything. Then I'd weed out the weeds and make an hour broadcast of it.

If you spoke as well as you write you would be the best talker in the English language. You almost certainly don't talk that well but with several hours of conversation, we could extract an hour that would make you sound eloquent.

I sound silly to myself saying it, but you owe a distant future without you, this much.

Regards,

Andy

E.B. White never succumbed and it's sad that we have no motion pictures of what he looked like or how he was but I always admired him for refusing to be interviewed. In 1963 Andy declined to go to The White House to accept a Presidential Medal of Freedom. I have often wished I had the same strength to resist being flattered by attention that my hero had.

An editor at Warner Books wrote a good letter asking me to contribute to a book they were going to publish called The Joy Of Pigging Out.

Patti Breitman
Editor
Warner Books

Thank you for your understanding letter. What you seemed to understand was that I probably wouldn't do what you were asking me to. That was good thinking on your part.

There is just so much Andy Rooney the world needs and having my name on the cover of a book and included in the publicity when I've had almost nothing to do with it, is the kind of step toward exceeding that need that I try not to take.

The Joy Of Pigging Out sounds like fun but I hope the phrase "pigging out" isn't past its prime. It reached its peak with teenagers about ten years ago and, if you're lucky, they may all be of book-buying age now and it won't occur to them, at least, that the phrase has been phased out of the lexicon of the current crop.

Good luck but don't wait for a contribution from me.

. . .

Mr. Steve Gelman
New Choices Magazine
New York, New York

Dear Mr. Gelman,

I did freelance magazine writing for years. Where were you when I needed you?

Thanks for the query about an article from me on "covert prejudice toward older people." Although it wouldn't stop me from writing it if I needed the money, as an old person myself, I haven't run into enough prejudice, overt or covert, to be turned on by the idea.

People are always giving me a break because I'm old and I hate them for it.

. . .

Sylvia St. Clair
New York, New York

Dear Ms. St. Clair,

I dislike the adult entertainment ads in the *West Side Spirit* where my column appears as much as you do but a writer cannot pull his column from every publication that prints something he disapproves of or there wouldn't be any place left to get it printed.

We're on the same side.

. . .

Dear Observant Viewer,

Thank you for calling my attention to the proper spelling of the word "Portuguese." I hope it will give you some confidence in the National I.Q., if not in mine, to learn that this form letter was made necessary by the fact that several hundred people joined you in pointing out my mistake.

I am contrite and have written:

IT IS P-O-R-T-U-G-U-E-S-E NOT P-O-R-T-U-G-E-S-E on the blackboard one hundred times.

Writers like to have their work read but poets are desperate to have someone read and appreciate what they have put down on paper. In spite of clear indications to the contrary, a great many poets think I'm a nice guy who will read and like the reams of unpublished—unpublishable—verse they send me.

Dear Penelope,

I've never written a Penelope and I'm sorry to have to tell you I don't care much for poetry even if it's good.

It's difficult enough to express a thought clearly using prose and I see no reason for anyone, with the possible exception of Byron and Shakespeare, to complicate the language further by being poetic.

I get sent a lot of terrible verse and the best I can say for yours is, it's several notches above average.

. . .

By coincidence, I got two letters the same day from two men in different parts of the country, complaining about the same thing. Mark Stuhlfaut of Plymouth, Minnesota and Bernard Brener of Sherman Oaks, California objected to conventional forms of salutations and endings in letters. They didn't approve of starting every time with "Dear" or ending with "Sincerely" and Mark wondered how "truly yours" someone really is who signs a letter "Yours truly.

In his letter, he envisioned a scene where he comes home from the office and greets his wife.

"Oh, honey," he says "I brought Jane home. She wrote me a letter saying she was very truly mine. Can I keep her?"

Bernard said "I wish you could do something on the nonsense involved in 'proper' letter writing where the polite forms of address are: 'My dear Mr.:' or 'Dear Sir:' etc. etc. and ending letters with 'Sincerely yours' or 'As always.'"

"Very few people I write to" Mr. Brener says "are 'My dear' anything, nor am I 'Sincerely' theirs.

"These high school proper letter-writing formalities should be put to rest" Mr. Brener concludes.

Dear Mr. Stuhlfaut and Mr. Brener,

While my inclination is to agree with you because those formalities in a letter seem silly sometimes, it's true of a lot of conventions we observe. If I could think of a better way to start and finish a letter, I'd do it but I can't.

Would we start simply "Ed" instead of "Dear Ed"? That wouldn't be much of an improvement.

Even if you don't like the person you're writing to, it's best to address him as "Dear" and even if you've been a little insincere, it's best to end it "Sincerely."

I personally never go any further than that though. I don't begin "My dear Mr. Smith" or end "Very sincerely," "Most sincerely" or "Sincerely yours." Just plain "Dear" and "Sincerely" is plenty for me.

Civilization has to lift itself by its own bootstraps. Politeness and civility do not always come naturally to us.

Every act that makes us more civilized, is worth preserving even if it's a little artificial.

So I appreciate getting your letters but I'm going to stick with "Dear" and "Sincerely." Maybe you two can become pen pals and call each other anything you want. Just be civil to each other.

Insincerely,

Someone is always tinkering with the English language. The president of a company called Better Education Thru Simplified Spelling, Inc. wrote to say "We hav enjoyed your comments. We feel that our ridiculous spelling system deserves some of the attention you could giv it.

"If s-o-n-g spells 'song' and l-o-n-g spells 'long,' then r-o-n-g should spell 'wrong.' Right? Wrong."

Mr. Citron went on to point out such inconsistencies in our use of "ent" and "ant" ending to words. We spell it "resid e-n-t" but it's "defend a-n-t," "presi d-e-n-t" but "attend a-n-t."

"We really aut to change our spelling" he says.

Abraham F. Citron
President

Dear Mr. Citron,

There's no question that our spelling could stand some revising. I'm willing to accept "thru," and "foto" and maybe even "fone" but I'd resist words like "wil," "giv," "nife" or "coud."

You're on much better ground arguing the inconsistency of "resident-tenant" or "president-attendant."

Lou Rakin was the bright, popular Stars and Stripes *staff member who edited the letters column called* B-Bag. *He was a lawyer and became a judge in New Jersey.*

Louis Rakin
Cranbury, New Jersey

Dear Lou,

Last night I spent more than an hour with the pages of the book idea you brought me and I'd like to give you a more lucid comment on them than I was able to do when you laid them on my desk.

You've done an incredible amount of work. It occurred to me that for all we saw of each other during the war, we knew each other hardly at all. I would not have known you could do what you did with this.

I have a friend, Dick Salant, a retired president of CBS News, who's been writing a book for eight years now. I asked his wife, Frannie, if she thought he was anywhere near finished with it.

"My God I hope not" she said. "I don't know what he'd do if he ever finished it."

I recognize some of this in you and hope you'll excuse me for calling it to your attention.

No one at a publishing house will read all the smoke you have blown. There is just so much proposing, outlining, planning and word processing you can do before you get down to writing a book. There are very few people in America who do not plan to write a book.

Your notion of a 1500 page book is out of the question unless you go to the vanity press and have it done with your own money.

I will send my friend at Random House everything you gave me.

Maurice P. O'Keefe Jr.
Atchison, Kansas

Dear Mr. O'Keefe,

Reaction to my comments was mixed but I was pleased to note that the spelling in the letters favorable to me was substantially better than in the critical ones.

. . .

Alfred Knopf, Jr.
Publisher
Atheneum

Dear Pat,

It's becoming increasingly difficult to be nothing but a writer. As soon as you have any success with it at all, people start pressing you to become something else. I've made some concessions and I haven't been thoroughly consistent but I don't intend to go the talk-show route with this book. I've seen too many people I admire hawking their wares and I ended up not admiring them as much as before.

I can imagine appearing on a television show in which the name of the book came up but I am not going to sit down with a public relations person and lay out an appearance schedule.

I've never thought publishers were very expert on how to sell books. I take publishers' advice on how to sell books about the way I take a butcher's advice on how to cook meat.

Look at it this way: if my book sells without them, it may rid you of this whole terrible talk-show mess publishers have gotten themselves into.

Regards,

The badly named And More By Andy Rooney, *published by Atheneum, sold more than 900,000 copies. Somehow I lost my resolve and when* My War *was published, I did my first "book tour." It was a better book but it sold 800,000 fewer copies than the book for which I did nothing.*

. . .

Lillian Bucellieni
Hot Springs, Arkansas

Dear Mrs. Bucellieni,

I liked your letter a lot but if you are just reading my book *Not That You Asked* you better get moving because that was three or four books ago. I'm writing them faster than you're reading them.

. . .

When it first came out, a woman wrote asking where she could find a copy of my book called My War.

Marie Lincoln
Roseburg, Oregon

Dear Marie,

Have you given any thought to a bookstore?

Roger Piantadosi
Washington Journalism Review

Dear Roger,

Bad taste though it may be, I can't resist telling you that I could hardly have been more pleased with your review of my book than if I'd written the review myself.

I admire writers who don't care what people say about their work but I am not among them. I care desperately. I consider myself a minor writer for this reason. J.D. Salinger is a major writer. He doesn't care. Of course, he doesn't write anything either.

. . .

Dick Stedler
Tonawanda, New York

Dear Dick,

Thanks for your suggestion.

I don't know what the solution is to the problem of long titles on small books unless it's to limit the number of letters in a book title the way they limit them in racehorse names. The max at the track is twenty-three.

That still wouldn't solve the problem for some of my books. Here's a thin one called *The Myth of American Eclipse*. There's barely room for that title longways with the book standing up, on the binding. The word "of" in the title would take all the room there is if it was printed across with the back standing up.

Anyway, thanks.

Charles McGrath
The New York Times Book Review
New York, New York

Dear Mr. McGrath,

For several months now I have been meaning to write you an angry letter and when I read your remarks about Joe Mitchell in Richard Severo's good obit of him, I thought I'd take the opportunity to ease into it that way.

Considering that I was never involved with *The New Yorker*, I knew a lot of people there. I had not known you were once on staff. Sandy Vanderbilt was a friend in London; I traveled in Germany during the war with Joel Sayre and shared a room in Cherbourg with Joe Liebling where, over a bottle of calvados, he espoused the advantages of dying at the peak of one's obituary value. I got to know E.B. White well. I visited him in North Brooklin during his last year when what he liked best was to have someone read to him from one of his books.

Joe Liebling and I had frequent lunches together after the war and one day he brought Joe Mitchell. We ate at an Italian restaurant, Villanova, near the *New Yorker* offices. Joe told me he thought Mitchell was "overrated" but he had things like that to say about a lot of people. On another occasion I had the lunch of a lifetime with Liebling, Andy White and Thurber, arranged by our mutual agent, Jap Gude. When Joe and I left the restaurant together, he said, referring to Thurber's blindness "The trouble with eating with him is, he never knows when you want to talk."

Am I eased in? Last September I was torn between hurt and anger over the dismissive review in your *Times Book Review* of a book I wrote, *My War*. My guess was that the review was written by someone too young to have known WW II or too busy to have read the book. Of thirty reviews from across the Country, it was the only negative one although the *Washington Post* reviewer complained about my treatment of Patton. I note that the two books *The Times* writer had reviewed previous to *My War* were *Knitting With Dog Hairs* and an authorized biography of Roy Rogers and Dale Evans. If you make the assignments, that gives me some idea of your estimation of my work.

The review was smug and snide, unusual for *The Book Review*. I understand perfectly well that it is bad form for a writer to send off a letter of this kind but the review still hurts and I couldn't keep myself from telling you.

Sincerely,
Andrew A. Rooney

. . .

Grover A. Ashcraft
Pierson, Florida

Dear Grover,

The manuscript of the book you wrote arrived and thank you for sending it but don't give me a test on what's in it. I get dozens of books a week and only read a few books a year. Editors and book publishers man the gates that stand between the millions of people who want to write books and the innocent reader. Editors decide what's good enough to be published. I don't read books that haven't passed this test.

You said in your letter that you are even ornerier than I am. I write to indicate otherwise.

The term "freelance," as used by writers, usually means "unemployed." After being discharged from the Army, I tried to make a living as a freelance magazine writer. I wrote about thirty articles and sold half of them.

I'd spend a month researching and writing a piece and send it to The Saturday Evening Post *or* Colliers, *hoping to sell it for $1,500. It would be sent back with a note from an editor saying how much they liked it but that they couldn't use it. Editors tried to be nice to freelance writers.*

I would send it to another magazine and then another and another of gradually diminishing circulation until it would finally sell to one that paid me $250 or $150 for my months work. And I was pleased to get it.

The end of my freelance magazine career came after I wrote this letter.

October 29, 1946

Mr. Frederick L. Allen,
Editor-in-Chief
Harper's Magazine

Dear Mr. Allen,

I have a strange story about an attempt to bomb New York City which I don't know what to do with but hoped to interest an editor in buying it.

My agent, Harold Ober, suggested that I might tell you the story in a letter. He said that he knew you well and thought you might be interested.

The story is this:

In November 1944, just before The Battle of the Bulge, I was sent back from Europe to work for two months in the *Stars and Stripes* office in New York. The second day back I boarded the crosstown shuttle in the New York subway and was surprised and pleased to see an old friend, also in uniform. He whispered to me in unconcealed excitement that he was working on the radar screen at Mitchell Field the previous day, Election Day, and a German submarine had launched a projectile towards New York City from its deck.

He had always seemed like a reliable person and his having been assigned to work in the radar control room was evidence that he had some expertise. According to his story he actually saw the missile en route but it had been either shot down or fell short for lack of power. German self-propelled V-1 bombs travelled at about 250 miles per hour and could be caught and shot down by our fighter planes. He said nothing else appeared on the screen so it had not been shot down.

We shuttled back and forth twice between Grand Central and Times Square while I listened to his story before I finally got off where I got on. I was skeptical but his story did not sound like anything he had made up. I went back to the office and called the AP. They knew nothing about it but they said they had heard the rumor. Subsequently, I realized they probably had not heard the rumor. That afternoon I went out to Mitchell Field and approached intelligence officers there. When I casually mentioned the incident to the colonel in charge there —I was a sergeant—he jumped up from behind his desk, closed the door and looked around furtively as though the place might have been wired.

"Look," he said, the way colonels said "look" to sergeants, "where did you hear this silly story? Don't repeat it." He was trying to shout at me in a whisper. "It isn't true, I don't know a thing about it. I don't even deny it."

I was convinced that something had happened.

The following morning *The New York Times* was eight pages deep in pure election news before it mentioned anything else. On page 19 there was a three-inch story with a Washington dateline which quoted War Department spokesmen as saying that, while "this is not a warning," robot attacks on either Washington or New York City "are entirely possible."

The timing was interesting and it was apparent that the War Department was afraid there would be panic in New York if people living there thought they were about to be bombed.

The next day I went back to Mitchell Field, in uniform, to look around. Overnight they had moved in most of the Army and Navy fighter plane strength from up and down the East Coast. No one I talked to would say why.

Because the story of any bombing—or attempted bombing—of New York was such an important one for the overseas soldier readers of *The Stars and Stripes*, I kept after it. I went to Washington and to the office of a Major General Bissell, at that time chief of Army Intelligence. There I got no farther than some colonel guarding the general's door. Where did I get my information? Who else had I told about it? Don't breathe a word of it to anyone and it's too absurd to talk about seriously.

Several weeks later, on January 8th, Admiral Ingram, the C-in-C of the Atlantic Fleet stated in a press conference that, "it is not only possible, but *probable*" that both New York and Washington would be the target of robot bomb attacks "within thirty to sixty days."

"The thing to do is not to get excited about it," the admiral said. "It might knock out a high building or two. It might create a fire hazard. It would certainly cause casualties in the limited area where the bomb might hit, but it could not seriously affect the progress of the war."

Immediately after the story of the Admiral's prediction started going out over the wires and on the radio, a War Department denial was issued.

"There is no more reason now to believe Germany will attack us with robot bombs than there was November 7, 1944," the statement said.

The denial, of course, was buried in the same column under Ingram's story in most morning papers. The reason it was issued so hurriedly, public relations officials admitted later was to stop or lessen the hasty exit thousands of people were making from New York and Washington on the already overcrowded transportation systems—planes, trains, buses. It was very serious.

By that time I was convinced the Germans had certainly made an attempt to bomb New York but even as a rumor I couldn't get it past censorship so I forgot about it and shortly after went back to Europe and rejoined the First Army press camp in Spa, Belgium.

The day after the war ended I was in Paris looking for almost anything to write about and it occurred to me the story might make a small box for the paper now that censorship on that sort of thing had been lifted. *The Stars and Stripes* printed the three-sentence story saying that there had apparently been an attempt made to bomb New York on Election Day, 1944. The idea of New York being bombed fascinated people.

The wire services picked up the story and it appeared on the front pages of most NY dailies. The War Department denied any knowledge of the story again and papers printed the denial, too.

I thought the story would end there without my ever knowing for sure what had happened.

More than a year later I returned to Germany as a civilian correspondent for *Cosmopolitan* magazine. It never occurred to me that I would have a chance to disinter the remains of the German U-boat story.

A few days before I was ready to come home I went out to the resort lake, Wannsee, and the luxury community there just outside Berlin. U.S. Army generals had taken over the fancy homes where Nazi leaders formerly lived. At one Army-run yacht club I got an

English speaking German, who was doing odd-jobs around the place, to take me on a tour of the lake. This young German had spent two years studying medicine at Columbia University before the war. We talked about a lot of things but you didn't usually ask someone like that what they did during the war. He was so voluble that I finally decided to ask.

"I started as an ordinary sailor," he said, "but I ended up as a submarine commander."

He was proud of two trips he had made to Japan in a 2000-ton freighter submarine carrying drugs which he had exchanged there for silk to be made into parachutes. He felt he was on safe ground talking with an American about those freighter trips to Japan because they hadn't involved any combat with the United States.

"There is something I've been wondering about for a long time," I said finally. "Maybe you'd know something about it. Did you people ever try to launch a rocket from the deck of a submarine against New York City?"

He did what so many Germans were doing. He launched into an explanation about how he hadn't really wanted to fight the war, that he liked Americans, that he was forced to fight. All of those things might have been true but I repeated the question and he finally said, very simply, "Oh, yes. As a matter of fact," he said a little proudly, "mine was one of the freighter subs in the Atlantic which was refueling the submarines lying off the coast of America.

"They had ramps set up on the decks of several submarines and they planned to hit both New York and Washington. They launched just one V–1 before they were caught by the Americans but they don't know what happened to the bomb.

"Their submarine was located with radar and somehow I think the Americans immobilized their ship with some sort of radio beams which interfered with their electric motors. They couldn't move and they were all captured alive. It was kept very secret."

Well, I don't know how accurate the details of his story are but he knew a lot and he knew of things like the launching ramps on the submarines that his ship was refueling.

Since I've returned from Germany I've gathered more confirmation of the attack on New York. Bill Gibson, a high school friend, who has written some short poetry for *Harper's*, has told me he was in the fighter control tower at Mitchell Field when they moved all the planes in there and he tells of the frantic action Fighter Command took to keep patrol planes in the air over New York night and day at the time.

My question: Is "WAS NEW YORK BOMBED?" a story you would be interested in for *Harpers?*

Mr. Allen wrote back to say he was interested. I rewrote the story with more details and it was published in Harper's. *I was paid $350 for months of work. It was at that point I knew I couldn't afford to be a freelance writer and eventually looked for work in television.*

PART SEVEN

Major and Minor Minorities

Walter Annenberg
Sunnylands
Rancho Mirage, California

Dear Mr. Annenberg,

Thank you for your informative and persuasive letter. I've been writing long enough to know how easy it is to make mistakes and how difficult it is to get all the right information and then understand it accurately.

You can protest for as long and as loud as you want to but people are always going to refer to that $50 million of yours as a "gift" to the United Negro College Fund and, while it is technically inaccurate, the spirit of it seems true enough and not worth quibbling about. You call it "a matching grant."

My basic argument with you is that I think the best hope for a better life for most American blacks lies in the prospect of their becoming assimilated into the mainstream of our society. Black colleges are inimical to this goal and it is for this reason that I don't think they should be encouraged.

Perhaps we'll meet someday—on which occasion I'll look forward to being castigated by you personally with as much charm as you displayed doing so in your letters to me.

You might be further irritated to know that I always confused your alma mater, The Peddie School, with Lawrenceville.

Ms. Riley worked for a Dallas newspaper but I do not have her first name.

Dear Ms. Riley,

Although I'm leery of anyone in the newspaper business except a salesman who carries a business card, I've come across yours in my desk a dozen times over the past months and always meant to send you the aborted *60 Minutes* piece I did on the Walter Annenberg promise of $50 million to the United Negro College Fund.

When I found your card, I could never find the piece—or vice versa. The two have surfaced from a pile on my desk at the same time and I'm fulfilling my promise.

Enclosed with it, is an article from last Wednesday's *Times* you may not have read. You'd be someone who is on the leading edge of black thought on these matters and it would be my guess that your opinions would coincide with those of the black leaders quoted in the article.

I find it depressing—worse, sickening. The idea of turning our backs on integration and returning to "separate but equal" is too sad to contemplate. It's as if we've lost. Twenty years ago I thought we were on our way to showing the world that the integration of the races was possible. It no longer looks as if it is and I am discouraged about the present and apprehensive about the future. How can it get any better? And it's terrible.

. . .

Brian Vieira
Brooklyn, New York

Dear Mr. Vieira,

I guess I was pretty lucky, after your how-dare-he letter to my boss, Don Hewitt, that he didn't fire me.

To tell you the truth, you weren't thinking clearly when you wrote it. The murders of Medgar Evers, Malcolm X and Martin Luther King Jr. were tragedies recognized by both white and black Americans but they had no deleterious effect on relations between the races. If anything, they pulled us together in common recognition of how terrible and sad those murders were. And pictures of Bull Connor, the redneck sheriff in his jackboots epitomized and made apparent to the world, including all of us, the attitude one segment of our population had toward blacks. It was not bad for race relations as you contend it was.

The O.J. Simpson verdict, on the other hand, has been overtly bad for race relations. There is already a hardening in the attitude many whites have toward affirmative action, for instance.

During the O.J. Simpson murder trial, I was criticized by his supporters for facetiously offering a one million dollar reward to anyone who found a murderer of Nicole Brown Simpson other than O.J.

Henry Bennett, Jr.
Newark, California

Dear Mr. Bennett,

When Emmett Till was murdered, I didn't have a million dollars but I'd be pleased to match my contribution to the fight against bigotry with yours, now or then, anytime.

I'm enclosing an early piece I wrote and produced for Harry Reasoner about Medgar Evers and his murderer, Byron de la Beckwith. See also your library for my hour documentary "Of Black America: Black History: Lost, Strayed Or Stolen," narrated by Bill Cosby.

Don't be rude without knowing what you're talking about.

For many years, CBS News regularly televised a one-hour broadcast documenting the events of the year just ending.

In 1989 I was assigned the job of writing and producing the hour. Broadcast on December 28th, it was an interesting and satisfying job that I did with my friend and editor, Bob Forte. It also came close to ending my career in broadcasting.

About halfway through the show, I wrote two paragraphs which seemed innocuous enough to me:

"There was some recognition in 1989, of the fact that many of the ills that kill us are self-induced. Too much alcohol, too much food, drugs, homosexual unions and cigarettes were all known to lead quite often to a premature death.

"The moral issue was this: If a person is repeatedly warned that something is damaging to his health and he continues to do what he knows is bad for him, is society responsible for his medical bills?"

The only complaint I anticipated was from some dissatisfied feminist who might have thought I should have used the politically correct "If a person is repeatedly warned that something is dangerous to his or her health . . . ."

The complaints were not from feminists but from the Gay and Lesbian Alliance Against Defamation. Their contention was that it was not homosexuality that made someone a potential victim of AIDS but unsafe sex. If I had written "Too much alcohol, too much food, drugs, unsafe sex . . ." they would have had no complaint.

In early January I was interviewed on the telephone by Chris Bull, a Vassar-educated reporter for a gay men's magazine, The Advocate. *The article appeared in February and in addition to suggesting I was homophobic, quoted me as having said that "blacks have watered-down their genes."*

It did not sound like anything I would ever have said to anyone who knew me and the suggestion that I was a racist was more hurtful than the suggestion that I was homophobic. I had been frequently enraged by what I saw of white behavior toward blacks. In the Army, I was arrested in St. Augustine when I boarded a bus designated to take soldiers back to Camp Blanding, and insisted on sitting at "the back of the bus" instead of the "white only" seats up front because the idea of a segregated bus infuriated me.

I wrote an episode in the series about black America called "Black History: Lost, Strayed or Stolen," narrated by Bill Cosby.

I had written a popular show for Lena Horne and Harry Belafonte called simply "Lena and Harry."

I suppose none of this proves I wasn't a racist but most people who knew my past would certainly have concluded that I was not. It was embarrassing to have to bring up all these things in my own defense.

Denying you have said something is useless because most newspapers reporting a story, repeat the damaging remarks and, at the bottom of the story say "Mr. Rooney denies having made the remarks." If Chris Bull had recorded my remarks and proved I said what he quoted me as saying, which I did not, I still would have denied I was a racist.

On February 8th, David Burke, president of CBS News, announced that he was suspending me for three months without pay.

After the Advocate *story was published, I wrote them a letter which they printed. It stands as evidence that, when attacked, it's better to just shut up. I didn't. I've even been advised not to reprint it here in this book.*

To Readers of the *Advocate*:

I'm sorry I offended so many homosexual people and would not be writing this if I were not sensitive to their complaints.

Many aspects of male and female homosexuality are puzzling to me. What part of men's and woman's homosexuality is based on their conscious decision to be gay or lesbian, and to what extent is it driven by forces beyond their control? Is it choice, or is it genetic, like being six feet tall, blue-eyed, or born with a cowlick?

With very little definitive medical or scientific evidence to go on, it seems to me that it is a behavioral aberration caused by some kind of trauma or caused when a male is born with an abnormal number of female genes, or vice versa. I'm thinking, for example, of the genes that produce hormones. Several male homosexuals I've talked with have challenged my interpretation of *normal* and explained to me their loving relationship with another man, which they consider normal. I appreciate all this and am even touched by it, but I do not consider homosexuality to be normal, even though I'm aware that the American Psychiatric Association has removed the diagnosis of homosexuality from its official list of mental illnesses. Is this evil of me?

It has been suggested that I'm prejudiced. In the sense that any conclusion, repeatedly arrived at with the thought processes, is prejudice when it starts coming to someone directly, shortcutting any further consideration of the subject, I confess to being prejudiced about a great many things. In regard to homosexuals, I think it's accurate to say you and I both know what we think and, to that extent, are prejudiced. We do not start over every time we're confronted with the subject.

Among the things I think about homosexuals—without thinking—is that they are, as a group, remarkably talented in an artistic sense and often with razor-sharp sensibilities. I am puzzled by this extraordinarily high percentage of artistically gifted gay people. I do not believe it is something that they have developed independent of their homosexuality. I believe it's inseparable from it. It may surprise you to know that I am regularly saddened to read of the death from AIDS of some young man who has risen to the top of his profession on the strength of his extraordinary ability.

Do I find the practice of one man introducing his penis into the anus of another repugnant? I do. Is it ethically or morally wrong and abnormal behavior? It seems so to me, but I can't say why.

I find the popular argument that it is the AIDS virus, not homosexuality, that kills, to be spurious. It's the same argument the gun-control lobby uses when it says it is criminals, not guns, that kill. The intelligent gay community has drastically reduced the incidence of HIV with what it calls "safe sex," but it fools itself into thinking it represents all the world's gay men.

I have a friend who, for many years, was one of the principal apologists for the tobacco industry. His logic was much the same too. He argued that it was lung cancer, not tobacco, that kills. It annoyed my friend that anyone would infer a direct connection between smoking and lung cancer, just as it annoys homosexuals to have people like myself deduce that homosexuality often leads to death by AIDS.

Homosexuals point to large numbers of nonhomosexual deaths from AIDS in Africa, just as my friend notes the number of nonsmokers who have acquired lung cancer. Of course nonhomosexuals who don't shoot drugs with dirty needles get AIDS.

My most intimate relationship with a homosexual was my forty-year friendship with Merle Miller. For young homosexuals who may never have heard of him, Merle was a first-rate novelist and the patron saint of the movement that brought gays out of the closet. In a landmark article he wrote in 1971 for the *New York Times Magazine* titled "WHAT IT MEANS TO BE HOMOSEXUAL," he pronounced, for all the world to read, his overt homosexuality. He was, he said, tired of being ashamed of it. Being homosexual stopped being a dirty secret that day of publication. I was proud to be his friend.

My friendship with Merle and a dozen other gay men taught me a lot about them and eliminated the know-nothing, all-American-boy kind of prejudice that I grew up surrounded by. I am most sympathetic to the homosexuals' argument that they have had to go on the offensive to keep from being on the defensive.

AIDS is a largely preventable disease, and I expressed the opinion that there is a growing public resentment about being taxed to pay for the health care of people suffering from self-inflicted diseases. Someone wrote and quoted me as saying in the broadcast that I thought homosexuals with AIDS should die. Do I strike you as someone who would say or even think such a terrible thing?

A New York lesbian quoted me as referring to "life-style" diseases, which I did not, and also quoted me as saying that society has a right not to pay the medical costs associated with them. I didn't say that, either. People don't listen. If she doesn't think a lot of people resent paying the medical costs of ills that might be avoided by intelligent behavior, she hasn't been reading the newspapers. But this is a public opinion, not my opinion. I'm the messenger.

Most victims—I think of gay men as victims and hope that doesn't further anger you—defend their homosexuality with such virulence these days that they make it sound like a virtue. Attacking is a way they have found to make themselves feel more comfortable. I understand that too. In my view, you're stuck with it, and you're doing what I'd do.

I'm genuinely sorry that homosexuals found the broadcast offensive, because it was not my intention to offend them. It was not my intention to make their already difficult gay life any more difficult.

I'll be more careful.

Sincerely,

Andrew A. Rooney

One of my most frequent correspondents is someone I've never met although I've come to think of him as a friend.

Wallace Bacon
Norwalk, Connecticut

Dear Wallace,

Of course I knew gays in the Army. Gays are under the impression they are incognito when it is almost always apparent to the most casual observer that they are gay. Do you know that? It always amuses me when gays think no one notices. We make instant, usually accurate, judgments about everyone we see. You can walk behind a person on the street without ever seeing a face and judge, accurately 90 percent of the time, that it is 1. a woman; 2. a person about fifty-three years old; and 3. someone with an education. I don't know what the signs are but when we feed them into our brain's computer, they turn out an answer unbidden.

You ask how I knew there were gays in the Army? Please.

Dear Wallace,

I was beginning to think you didn't like me anymore.

You said you had an old letter of mine in hand but I don't recall ever saying I was ignorant on the subject of homosexuality and I never confused you with my old friend and classmate who died two years after declaring his homosexuality and leaving his wife and children in the small town where he had practiced medicine.

Your theory that nature or God may have intervened to cut back on the population explosion by recently giving us a large homosexual community doesn't hold water. It wouldn't hold anything. Why would God have waited until people screwed up so much of the world before intervening and making elements of the population indifferent to the kind of sex that produces so many babies?

Would it be a violation of the position you take on sexual preference in the letters you so often write me, if you got a typewriter?

Write me again and tell me what you're doing—in three or four years.

. . .

Dear Mr. Sergeant,

Because you are not the only one who thought so after reading my column, I must have given the impression that, as you say, I am "anti-Indian." I am not. I am anti-gambling and believe that too many American Indians have sold their glorious heritage to a handful of big time international hustlers who are using Indians as a front for their casino operations.

They don't call it gambling anymore, by the way. Every single angry letter or fax I got from the representative of a tribe called it "gaming." They must have got together, on the advice of a public relations company, and decided "gaming" sounded better than "gambling." Gaming makes it sound as if the suckers who do it have a chance to win.

Naturally you frightened me by indicating you sent a copy of your letter to my boss. I'll bet I'll be hearing from him. He may even fire me when he has time although I think he's too busy this week. I happen to know his wife is doing over their living room.

Several readers were so mad at me, they wrote my boss's boss. I hardly dare write anything of a controversial nature anymore for fear someone will write to the boss of my boss's boss.

Have a good day.

Elaine Schuster
Southfield, Michigan

Dear Ms. Schuster,

I don't know what you do for a living but you might consider writing angry letters full time. You do it very well. Of all the letters I got condemning me for what I said about Indians, none was so judicious and effective as yours. "She's got me there," I thought to myself several times as I read it.

Barry Goldwater
Scottsdale, Arizona

Dear Barry,

It was great to hear from you. Considering we live, and have lived, in two different worlds and I didn't vote for you in 1964, it's surprising how often I think of you. I wanted to say something when you were married and didn't know what to say but I thought of you then.

Your going-away party in Washington was memorable. I often laugh at your unlikely friend, Teddy Kennedy's remark about you.

He said "Barry's motto has always been 'Ready! Shoot! Aim!"

You say you're eighty. I had my seventy-fourth birthday last Thursday and I wish I could get death out of my mind. I'm having too good a time to die but I understand it may happen. I'm sure it's occurred to you. In spite of a statement I heard you make to the contrary, you will never be forgotten. When you retired from the Senate, you said "No one'll know who I am a couple of years from now." That's about as wrong as you get although you've made a lot of statements about which I feel to the contrary.

I get to Scottsdale every so often and when I come again, I'm going to alert you and insist that we have dinner together at one of my favorite places in the whole country, Los Olivos. You must come to New York and if you're ever there without an engagement, we'll take you to one of the twenty best restaurants in the world. Nine of them are in New York.

Last year I got in big trouble with your Indians. I said some things I shouldn't have said—you know how that is. You're an expert at it. I said and I still think, that the best thing the Indians could do for themselves would be to join the Country. It's not a bad Country to be a part of. I said (how could I have said this?) that they were great at living on the land and they wove cloth and made nice jewelry but had no significant music or literature of their own. I pointed out they hadn't even used the wheel before the Europeans got here. I also said that the phrase "Native American" is not accurate. They are no more "native" than the rest of us although they did get here a few thousand years earlier across the Bering Strait. From the snowfall of mail I got, I might as well have attacked Mother Teresa.

I know I shouldn't have said it but the proliferation of gambling casinos angers me. The Indians are just being used. They don't really own or operate the casinos. The something-for-nothing idea behind it is a bad influence on the whole Country.

I talk to Bill Leonard all the time, usually interrupting one of those endlessly inane conversations you ham radio operators conduct over the airwaves.

Warm regards,

Andy

After the singer Kurt Cobain committed suicide, I made some unkind remarks on 60 Minutes. *Although that broadcast has a reputation of appealing primarily to older Americans, some younger people must watch because I received more than 10,000 angry letters from viewers under thirty years old.*

Tom Stevens
Lakewood, Colorado

Dear Mr. Stevens,

You say, "It is clear from the news accounts that Kurt Cobain suffered from terminal Manic Depression."

That was not clear in any news account I read. Had I thought that was his problem, my attitude would have been different. I've known people who did suffer from Manic Depression and have nothing but sympathy for them. Judging from the simple middle-of-the-night kind of black thoughts we all have, I can imagine what it might be like to be afflicted with the disease and feel that way day and night. My friend Mike Wallace suffered from depression for about six months and he often talks about the terror of it.

Your letter makes the unsubstantiated assumption that Cobain suffered from Manic Depression and then supports your argument with valid details from your own tragedy.

I do not mean to demean Kurt Cobain or to make light of any person's death but his suicide at age twenty-seven angers me. I'd like to have the years left that he had left. It is apparent from what I've read now that he was talented and his death is a tragedy but if we all agree that life is good and death is not then no successful person in good health who takes his own life is a sensible person. It makes me suspicious of his music. If Kurt Cobain applied the same thought process to his music that he applied to his drug-infested life, then it's reasonable for a reasonable person to think that his music may not have made sense either.

One of Kurt's fans, a young woman named Renae Ely stood outside his home in Seattle with tears streaming down her face, according to the story. "It's hard to be a young person nowadays" she said. "He helped open people's eyes to our struggles." Please, Renae, wipe away the tears. You're breaking my heart. I'd love to relieve you of all the pain you're going through by switching my age for yours.

The band, Nirvana, is said to have "pulled away from the synthetic sound of much of rock music." The band dressed in old clothes apparently bought in thrift shops. The suggestion was that the clothes were ultimately casual and natural. The picture in the paper is of Kurt Cobain in a pair of ragged jeans with a hole in the knee. I doubt that Kurt Cobain ever prayed or did the kind of work that would have worn a hole in his pants. The pants look to me as though they were carefully made by an expensive tailor, who built a hole in the knee, in order to make them look old and worn.

On a back page of the same newspaper where Kurt Cobain occupied space on page one was a short obituary of Samuel E. Thorne who died at the age of eighty-seven. Professor Thorne was a retired legal historian at the Harvard Law School.

"Mr. Thorne" the obituary said, "was an authority on English legal history dating to the 12th Century who wrote extensively on the subject.

"During World War II he was a Navy cryptanalyst in the Pacific. In addition to his son, Samuel, he is survived by his wife of 50 years and another son, Stuart."

The length and positioning of the obituaries notwithstanding, I think Professor Thorne made better use of his life than Kurt Cobain made of his.

Conor K. McFarren, MB
Dept of Psychiatry
New Haven, Connecticut

Dear Dr. McFarren,

I'm going to give you the benefit of the doubt and assume the "MB" after your name was either a misprint or that you British have some arcane alphabetic designation for doctor.

Were I grading your letter, as you must grade your students, I'd give it a C+. It was earnest, grammatical, impeccably spelled and indicated you have read all your lessons. On the minus side, you used an unnecessary number of words to express a few simple ideas. This is a common failing among scientists, sociologists and medical people, particularly those in psychiatry. It springs from a deeply-rooted desire of an individual to give the impression of more intellect than exists.

My evaluation of my work and myself does not vary a whit from the value of either. Of course I was comparing Kurt Cobain's death with my own. I said as much but I am more afraid that on the occasion of my demise editors will judge me on page one as a television celebrity, not in back as a writer who did what he could with what he had. That depends some on the distance of my demise from the apex of my celebrity. There are some disadvantages to dying at the peak of one's obituary value. I hope to outlive mine and die quietly on page 27.

But thanks for writing.

PART EIGHT

Thanks But No Thanks

Robert Reid
Chicago Tribune

Dear Bob,

It seems like a lot to ask me to speak to a local chapter of the National Conference of Christians and Jews for nothing but the honor of it when I am neither and when the person asking for my services has denied himself the availability of my column for his newspaper.

A few weeks ago I went to Dallas to speak at the AP Managing Editors convention which seemed worthwhile but, as a general rule, I don't do local chapters of anything.

If you'd like me to, I'll write to Tom O'Donnell and tell him I can't come. If you want to tell him yourself, feel free to use one of the effective excuses I often employ:

1. My wife and I have been planning a trip to Paris and I will be out of the Country on March 9th. (This has served me well many, many times.)

2. March 9th is my birthday (or 35th anniversary etc.) and my children have planned a big surprise party for me that I know all about so I can't come.

3. I'm terribly sorry but I have a previous speaking engagement with an IBM banquet on Marcos Island (The Homestead, the Del Coronado in San Diego, Hilton Head etc.).

4. My contract with CBS (Acme Speakers Bureau etc.) prevents me from accepting any outside speaking engagements. I sincerely wish this

were not the case because there's nothing I'd rather do than speak to (name of group) but my hands are tied. I hope you'll understand.

Try any of those.

I feel bad about it but speaking to a local chapter of the National Association of Christians and Jews doesn't seem like the way I ought to be spending that weekend.

As a bit of trivia for you, I knew the man, Everett Clinchy, who changed the name of the organization from The National Association of Jews and Christians to the National Association of Christians and Jews when he became head of it in the late 1950s.

Impress your friends with that tidbit of information at the dinner.

. . .

Ms. Laura Inciardi
Norwalk, Connecticut

Dear Ms. Inciardi,

Thank you for the invitation to speak at your Secretary's Day lunch on April 27th but my wife and I have planned a trip to Paris on that date.

I might also say that I'm ambivalent about Secretary's Days. It always seemed to me a good secretary would prefer a raise to the praise.

Dear Mr. Ryan,

Thank you and your seniors for inviting me to speak at your graduation ceremonies but my wife and I have planned a trip to France which coincides with that date.

My wife taught at the Thomas School for eleven years and, while we would be saddened to see the name "Thomas" disappear into oblivion, when the King School and Low-Heywood absorbed The Thomas

School, too, and became "King & Low-Heywood-Thomas Schools" I was ready to give up on saving names. "The King, Low-Heywood, Thomas School is not a name you can live with for long. What a challenge for a school cheerleader!

When I read of the woman named Worthington recently, who married a man named William Traendly, and wanted to keep her own name, she became Mrs. William Worthington-Traendly. What ever will happen if her daughter, named, perhaps, Nancy Worthington-Traendly, meets a boy she wants to marry, named Roger Whittley-Wilson? If Nancy wants to keep her own name, she's got a problem. She would become Mrs. Roger Worthington-Traendly-Whittley-Wilson, the Third, perhaps. That's nothing though, compared to what the next generation would face if they too, had parents who had kept their original names and hyphenated them with the name of the person they married.

That's where The King & Low-Heywood-Thomas Schools finds itself—or selves.

Lora Wiley
Producer
The Magic Hour
Burbank, California

Dear Ms. Wiley,

Thank you for your letter proposing an appearance by me on *The Magic Hour*. I am excited about the prospects of doing it and of appearing on your show. It could be the break I've been waiting for.

It looks as though we'll be able to tape the segment next Tuesday, June 29th and get it to you in Burbank the following morning.

My fee will be $50,000 plus expenses—unless I have to read the script you sent me in which case the charge would be $100,000.

Deborah Raffin is a tall, beautiful, semi-famous actress who ran a business called Dove Audio with her husband, Michael Viner.

When I recorded parts of my book Sweet and Sour *for them, Deborah stood in the control room as I read, giving me advice and direction. I was much impressed and surprised that anyone as good-looking as she was, was so competent.*

Deborah and Michael branched out into other enterprises and approached me with the idea of a situation comedy. I thought the idea was to use material in my columns as the basis for the plots from week to week. I didn't have any idea how they could do that and my basic attitude was "Fine. Go ahead and do it. Send me the money."

Michael Viner, Deborah Raffin
Beverly Hills, California

Dear Deborah, Michael,

While I'm flattered by your attention and interest in my work, I cannot honestly say I'm enthusiastic about the concept of a sitcom called *Andy*.

When I originally agreed that it would be interesting to have someone do something with my essays, I was thinking of the essays, not of me as a character. I may have made the mistake of being too confident that someone would think the material would stand on its own. I could simply not bring myself to be involved as you've involved me in your idea sheets. If there were to be a character even vaguely taken from my persona, I wouldn't want my name visible anywhere on the credits. Presumably this would diminish your interest in the project to somewhere down around none at all.

I think you make a mistake in developing this by thinking first of an actor to play the lead role. That might be important for selling it but it wouldn't sustain it. What the project needs is writers. For all my respect for you as an actress Deborah and my creeping affection for you as a person, it is my long held opinion that actors are a dime a dozen—even pretty good pretty ones. There are fifty producers, directors and actors standing around waiting for one writer to put something down on paper so they can change it.

You are obviously people who know how to do things and get them done but I'm not interested in being a road company *Dave*.

. . .

Lukas Barr
SPY Magazine
New York, New York

Dear Mr. Barr,

To what end for me would I submit to a lie detector test for a story in *SPY Magazine*? Would it make me rich and famous? Win me friends I don't have? Make me thinner, younger, smarter? Why would I spend my time doing that for an organization I don't work for and whose publication I have never read?

I hold some petty opinions in my heart that my brain wishes were not there. I don't know how a polygraph machine would read my answers to questions about those things. An honest response on my part might offend some people and I don't give dishonest answers so I prefer not to be put in the position of having to answer them.

Sincerely, (but check that)
Andrew A. Rooney

James Coppersmith
WCVB
Needham, Massachusetts

Dear Jim,

Emily passed on your invitation for me to speak at the Worcester Business Expo on October 16th.

I do what Emily asks me to do but there are some things the organizers should know before they say they definitely want me there.

While it's not my favorite thing to do or even anything I do very well, I could speak to this group. I am, however, not enthusiastic about appearing at 10 A.M. "to mingle with Worcester's business leaders." It is neither Worcester nor business leaders I object to, it's appearing and mingling. I'm a terrible appearer and mingler. Fifteen minutes of mingling is all I can take.

You suggest I would also "open the Expo." Compared to my opening of Expos, I'm a great mingler and appearer. I'll go even further. I don't open Expos. I don't know what it entails but I don't cut ribbons, hit bows of boats with bottles or otherwise perform ceremonial duties.

Emily would not have given me your invitation had she not hoped I'd do it. I know the respect she has for you so I accept your invitation as long as you understand that I don't have a salesman's bone in my body.

It's difficult to understand why anyone who has ever seen me on television would think I could be paid to say something but I get frequent requests to do commercials. Shortly after my first commentary for 60 Minutes, *an advertising agency offered me money to read their commercial for aspirin. They admitted that I was their choice because they felt my, whiney, nasal voice was perfect for the product.*

I regularly turn down or ignore requests for me to do commercials.

Robert H. Taupeka
Emperor Clock Company
Fairhope, Alabama

Dear Mr. Taupeka,

Thank you for your letter and I am interested in your offer for me to be the radio and television spokesman for the Emperor Clock Company. You must need a spokesman because I have never heard anyone speak of an Emperor Clock.

You probably understand that to do this I'd have to resign my position at CBS News and give up my newspaper column with the Tribune Syndicate. To compensate for these losses, I would not consider starting negotiations with your company for a figure less than $30 million for the first year with a guarantee of a minimum of five years. If you are interested in this proposition, please write or call at your earliest convenience and I will ask my lawyer to get together with your financial people and have them mail me the money.

I look forward to a long association that could prove to be beneficial for both of us and a new day when people like me would have heard of an Emperor Clock.

Joel Shukovsky
Producer, *Murphy Brown* Show
Hollywood, California

Dear Joel,

Thanks. I'm flattered and tempted by your invitation to appear on an episode of *Murphy Brown*. The show is very well done and I enjoy watching it. I'm impressed by the writing and I haven't been so taken by the beauty of a woman as I have been by Candice's since I fell in love with Donna Reed when I worked at MGM in 1946.

But I'm not going to do it. It just seems wrong. When a writer reads something someone else has written, he becomes an actor. I don't want to be an actor.

. . .

The Anchorage Times

To The Editor,

In the past month since my trip to Alaska, I've had numerous friendly and unfriendly letters about my behavior. Several of them enclosed a clipping of a letter you published and I'd like to respond to it.

I accepted the invitation months ago from the Alaska Press Association to speak at their annual dinner in Anchorage. Their representative said they couldn't afford to pay me but would pick up my airfare. I had always wanted to come to Alaska and this seemed like a good way to get a free trip.

When we arrived at the hall, I was surprised to see that they were selling tickets at the door for $25. I had spoken several times to the organizer about not wanting television cameras recording my talk. My attitude may be hard to explain and you may not accept it anyway but this is it.

1. I write for a living. It seemed wrong to me for a television company to come in and tape forty-five minutes of my material which they planned to broadcast with no payment to me. They were not looking for excerpts for a news report.

While I was willing to work for the press group gratis I was not willing to do it for commercial television.

2. I intended to say some critical things about the direction journalism has taken in recent years. My remarks were intended for my peers in the business not for the public. The public is already critical enough of the media.

3. I am not a good speaker. I invariably get nervous to the point of nausea before a speech. Staring at a television camera for an hour exacerbates this condition.

4. I'm sorry I disappointed the audience by walking out on the spur of the moment but it seemed like the right thing to do at the time.

The following night I spoke in Fairbanks and we had a grand time there.

. . .

Half a dozen letters a week come to me from people asking if I will please write a note congratulating their parents on having been married for thirty-eight years or congratulating their son for having been made an Eagle Scout. You have to like these kind people but they don't understand.

Timothy B. Dosemagen
Boy Scouts
Highland Park, Illinois

Dear Mr. Dosemagen,

Thank you for your invitation to speak at your Boy Scout dinner in Highland Park, Illinois.

I will be unable to attend.

I hope your event is a success.

JulieAnn Rico,
Palm Beach County Bar Association
West Palm Beach, Florida

Dear Ms. Rico,

Thank you for your invitation to speak to the Palm Beach County Bar Association luncheon meetings on either August 6, 1992, December 10, 1992, March 11, 1993, June 10, 1993 or at a dinner meeting January 21, 1993 or April 8, 1993. Unfortunately, I'm busy that day.

Inasmuch as you say your budget does not provide for an honorarium, please call when your members stop accepting fees for their services and I'll be right down.

PART NINE

Who's Watching

One morning I set out with a camera crew to go to Pottstown, Pennsylvania, noted on the label of any of the products called MRS. SMITH'S PIES, *as their place of manufacture, to see if we could actually find "Mrs. Smith."*

We could not, of course. It made a funny piece for 60 Minutes *but some of the residents of Pottstown, whose economy depends a lot on the baking factory, were angry. A reporter for a publication called* The Mercury, *wrote a disparaging review which was later rewritten by another reporter for* The Philadelphia Inquirer.

Mr. Shandy Hill
The Mercury
Pottstown, Pennsylvania

Dear Shandy,

I'm tempted to be touched by your defense of "Mrs. Smith" but I suspect Pottstown's anger emanates more from the pocketbook than from the heart.

Large corporations are practicing a mild form of deceit when they take over small, family-run businesses with good names and then keep the name but change the product. That was the point of my piece on *60 Minutes*.

In both your columns you fudge the tense. Yes, I knew there *was* a Mrs. Smith and I know there *is not* a Mrs. Smith. It is not the canard you claim it to be to say "there is no Mrs. Smith" when you are talking about "Mrs. Smith's Pies."

It irritates me when a company like Kellogg's takes Mrs. Smith's name, commercializes the product and then retains the homey-sounding "Mrs. Smith" as though she was still baking the pies in her kitchen. Kellogg's has a perfectly good name of its own and should use it on its pies—which I understand are also good.

Amanda Smith must have been quite a woman but I'll bet she wouldn't like it any better than I do to find her name on a pie containing, among other things, "partially hydrogenated soybean oil, skim milk, lecithin, mono- and diglycerides, artificial flavor and color and vitamin A palmitate."

I have a good feeling Amanda Smith would be on my side.

. . .

Over the years, I've been on some wild goose chases. Companies are often more secretive than governments.

Lisa McCarren
Scott Paper Co.
Philadelphia, Pennsylvania

Dear Ms. McCarren,

I'm pleased you wrote offering your help in supplying information for my newspaper column.

For some time now I have been trying to document the gradual diminution of the actual content of rolls and boxes of paper products.

Does Scott Paper make available the changes in roll sizes and box contents of the products it has on the market along with the changing prices?

We are interested in comparing, for example, the actual paper content of a box of tissues in 1992 with the comparable box sold any year in the 1960s.

When did Scott begin producing paper tissues and what was the size of an individual tissue at that time as compared with one of their tissues today?

We would like to make the same comparison with rolls of paper towels and rolls of toilet paper. Any information you can give me along these lines would be appreciated.

Was it strange I never got the information?

. . .

Manufacturers of everything keep putting less of the product in their boxes. I complained when I noted that there were 15 ounces in a box of Sun-Maid raisins.

Mr. Barry F. Kriebel
Sun-Maid Growers
Kingsburg, California

Dear Mr. Kriebel,

I was interested in the information and pleased to get the covers from the old boxes of raisins. While you may be right that because 15 ounces is two cups and "... most common recipes call for either one cup or 1½ cups" Sun-Maid decided many years ago to pack them in weight increments that made cups.

If that's true the two box covers you sent were poor evidence of it. Both recipes on the 1915 box called for raisins in pounds, not cups.

But I like Sun-Maid raisins and don't think any harm was done.

Jim Hoskinson
New Canaan, Connecticut

Dear Jim,

You're a troublemaker.

Your complaint about the apparent fallacy in my report on divorce statistics moved me to look into the matter further and, after some research I am unclear about whether you're right or wrong. You would be unclear too if you had looked into it further.

The basic problem with divorce statistics is that no one, including the Census Bureau, knows how many *married* people there are in the United States. They may know how many have *been* married but not how many are alive and married now, for the first and only time. Without that figure there's no way to arrive at a divorce rate.

The people I spoke to in Washington were insistent that the *projected* divorce rate for all marriages taking place in 1992 is 50 percent. Projecting is easier than counting because it's guessing.

I'm enclosing a few dregs of research and I don't ever want to hear from you again on this matter.

Otherwise, warm regards.

. . .

Peter Diamondopoulos
Adelphi University
Garden City, Long Island

Dear Mr. Diamondopoulos,

In going through a pile of stuff on my desk too good to throw away but not important enough to do anything about, I came on your letter that did not call for an answer. The last letter I got from a college president was from the one at Las Vegas-Nevada. He was angry with me over some slighting reference I'd made to scholarship there.

After they had won the NCAA championship, I wrote that I rated the academic excellence of a college in inverse ratio to the success of its basketball team. He took offense. By this standard of mine Adelphi rates very high indeed. I note you have won fewer than a quarter of your games this year.

. . .

In 1978 I was in Washington doing a short television report on the great number of organizations that have their headquarters there. The American Association of Retired Persons had its name carved in stone across the top of its building and the cameraman was photographing that when someone emerged from the building and ordered us to stop. I thought that was strange and decided to look further into an organization I knew nothing about, the AARP. They did everything they could to keep us from the facts.

A member of one of the country's most prominent law firms, representing the AARP, wrote a letter to the president of CBS News, Richard Salant, hoping to discourage the broadcast. Salant forwarded the letter to me to answer.

Mr. Stuart Robinowitz
Paul, Weiss, Rifkind, Wharton & Garrison
New York, New York

Dear Mr. Robinowitz,

On several occasions recently I have heard statements that apparently originated from AARP Headquarters or those of Colonial Penn Insurance Company, suggesting that the report I am doing on the relationship between the retired people associations and the insurance group has not been done according to the highest journalistic standards.

These suggestions are personally disturbing and professionally damaging to me. Your letter to the president of CBS News, in advance of the broadcast of the report, indicating that it may be inaccurate because of "the manner in which this program was produced," is a serious charge.

To state that I set out to make this report with any intention except to ascertain the facts of the matter is wrong. I make my living as a writer and a reporter. I am in no doubt about the ethical standards of my profession and am not ambivalent about my determination to stand by them. To say that I have only gone to sources who have a negative attitude toward the relationship between the AARP and Colonial Penn ignores the fact that I made repeated attempts to film interviews with the principals, Leonard Davis, the originator of the plan to use the AARP as a sales tool for Colonial Penn, Cyril Brickfield, president of the AARP and John MacWilliams, president of the insurance company.

My report on the AARP was broadcast and it forced major changes in the organization, they dropped Colonial Penn as their insurance company and signed on with Prudential. In 1996, I read that the AARP was ending that association and taking on a new insurance company and couldn't resist reviewing the experience I'd had doing the 60 Minutes *report in a column.*

The headline most newspapers used was:

THERE'S GOLD IN THE OLD

The text follows:

There's big money in old folks if you get enough of them to buy your product. No organization knows this better than the AARP, the American Association of Retired Persons, with thirty-five million members.

I'm plenty old enough to belong to the AARP—they've reduced the age requirement to fifty—but I've never joined. I'm prejudiced against the AARP because of the bad start it got. People tell me all that is in its dark past and I know it's unfair but my negative feeling about the gigantic association won't go away.

The AARP was started in 1958 by an insurance salesman named Leonard Davis after he met an elderly woman named Ethel Percy Andrus who had been working to help teachers with medical insurance through an organization called The National Association of Retired Teachers.

David recognized a good thing when he saw it and realized the market for insurance sales to old people wasn't limited to teachers. He wanted to expand it to include "persons" so he put up $50,000 to establish the AARP.

This was not an eleemosynary institution. Andrus's interest was old people; Davis's interest was money. He put together the Colonial Penn Insurance Company which he made certain, through several legal maneuvers, was in firm control of the AARP. He then started using it, through its magazine *Modern Maturity*, as a sales tool for insurance policies.

Leonard Davis made hundreds of millions of dollars from the sale of insurance policies to AARP members. For several years, Colonial Penn was the single most profitable company in the United States even though the policies it sold to AARP and NRTA members were rated "poor."

Davis's plan was a deviously ingenious sales scheme. The AARP was not much more than a front for the insurance company. At local AARP meetings around the country, volunteers set up desks to sell insurance. They didn't even have to pay salespeople. They conned members into thinking they were doing charitable work. The AARP office in Washington did not even have a list of its own members. That membership was kept under lock and key in the offices of the Colonial Penn Insurance Company.

After a *60 Minutes* report exposing all this was broadcast in 1978, the AARP got rid of Colonial Penn and signed up with the Prudential Insurance Company.

Just last week the AARP ended its eighteen-year association with Prudential and has given its $4 billion contract to the United Health Care Corporation. I know nothing about the arrangement except you can bet that the AARP will be taking a 3 percent kickback from every single premium its members pay. Nothing illegal there. It's just that I still have a bad taste in my mouth.

People have told me of the good things the AARP does and I believe them. Cyril Brickfield, a lawyer and an important part of the Leonard Davis machine that so efficiently ran the AARP for its own profit, finally left a few years ago with an exit fee so large the AARP won't say what it was.

The AARP's current executive director is a former Catholic priest and longtime AARP employee named Horace Deets. He was hired twenty years ago by Harriet Miller, then the director, who was fired when she openly disapproved of what Leonard Davis was doing.

She won a $445,000 lawsuit against the AARP and is now, of all things mayor of Santa Barbara, California. Leonard Davis lives in Florida. I don't think they exchange greeting cards.

People speak highly of Deets but I am not at ease with anyone who accepted the heavy hand of Leonard Davis for so long.

The most prickly thorn in the AARP's side now is Sen. Alan Simpson. The AARP enjoys tax exemption and nonprofit mailing privileges that amount to millions of dollars a year and Simpson has tried to have them taken away. He claims that AARP publications and mailings are ads for their many business enterprises and should be taxed and that their mailings should bear stamps like any other for-profit company's mail.

The AARP does have a lot of income-producing sidelines. As a small example, AARP members get a reduced rate if they rent a car from Hertz or Avis and the AARP, in turn, collects 5 percent of what members pay the rental company. It's still a good deal for members.

Simpson's opponents claim his is a political vendetta being waged against the AARP because he feels the organization has generally supported Democratic causes. In view of this criticism which they don't want to spread and ruin their lobbying efforts in Congress, the AARP has been neutral to the point of paranoia during the current Presidential race.

Maybe I'll join the AARP when they lower the age limit to forty-five.

You can understand why the current AARP management wasn't pleased and I got an angry letter from a representative which I answered.

James R. Holland
American Association of Retired Persons
Washington, D.C.

Dear Mr. Holland,

While I understand why you disliked my column looking into the American Association of Retired Persons' not-so-distant past, I thought the occasion of a change in its insurance connection was good reason to remind people of what it had been so that they might be wary of it in the future. Wary is all I suggest.

My experience reporting on the AARP in 1978 was one of the most memorable of my life—that's a life that included three years reporting WW II. What the AARP was doing for the first thirty or so years of its existence is not something I'll forget nor do I think current members should be unaware of it.

The AARP's behavior in those years was despicable, dishonest and unforgiveable. It seems likely that things have changed but I would want to start all over and have a close look at all aspects of the operation before I could endorse it.

Your suggestion that the AARP has turned itself into an eleemosynary institution is persuasive. I hope you are right and I am anxious to believe you. There certainly is a need for what the AARP purports to be.

. . .

Except for abortion and what time to go to bed at night, there are few subjects on which Americans are more divided than they are on guns. In 1991, former President Reagan favored a seven-day waiting period for anyone wanting to buy a gun. I commented on it and, predictably got angry letters.

Bill Huddy
KQSB
Santa Barbara, California

Dear Bill,

Thanks for the kind words.

We had a huge reaction—thousands of letters and they ran more than ten to one in my favor. The people who hated it were divided between gun advocates—"They had a right to have those weapons"—and the religious right.

Fortunately, when I referred to "religious nuts" the Catholic nuts thought I was talking about the Jehovah's Witnesses, the Baptists thought I meant the Quakers, the Jews thought I was talking about the

Muslims and the Muslims probably thought I meant the Episcopalians. Everyone thought I was talking about someone else.

I've spent most of the week going to lunches and dinners honoring Mike Wallace on the occasion of his 75th birthday. He could start a plaque museum.

I did a brief report for television about the rest stops along the New York State Thruway and had some contact with a Marriott executive because Marriott was rebuilding them.

Paul Gaiser
Marriott Corporation
Washington, D.C.

Dear Mr. Gaiser,

I've been watching your rest stop buildings go up on the New York State Thruway and, while they look very good, I'd prefer that you had staggered their construction so that all the rest stops along the 500 miles of the road were not closed at the same time. This has prevented hundreds of thousands of us who use the Thruway from looking forward to a place to stop and rest.

Your estimate that your new restaurants and rest stops "usher in a new era in road travel" may be a little effusive but if the mens' rooms are clean and the coffee hot it will be a step in the right direction.

I compare all highway facilities in America with the ones along major highways in France. If the restaurants there were anywhere in Washington, D.C., they'd be the best restaurant in town. Perhaps your people should go over and study them with an eye toward imitation. The bread alone would change my attitude toward driving here.

Dear Mr. Powell,

It was apparent to me that what I said about veterans' benefits would not be popular with professional veterans but I was careful to exclude disabled or handicapped veterans from my opinion that America doesn't owe the average ex-serviceman anything. Veterans got what they had coming to them: a free Country.

How can you twist what I said as you did in your letter? You say I "picked on Itzhak Perlman . . . by raising the question of whether or not" he's the best violinist in the world. I raised no such question. My first sentence reads "Itzhak Perlman is the best violinist in the world." Is that a question Mr. Powell?

You say that I would not be eligible to receive VA health care. If that's true, you know something I don't. I served four years in the U.S. Army. What I said was "any veteran 65 or older can get free treatment for any ailment at any veterans' hospital." Is that true or false? I'm not talking about out-patient care or nursing homes. It is my understanding that at age 65 a veteran will be admitted to a Veterans' Hospital. Tell me I'm wrong and you'll be wrong.

. . .

Environmental Group One
Connecticut

Dear Ms. Wood,

Thank you for your letter. It sounds worthwhile and inasmuch as you've asked for suggestions, I'll offer one that might help your efforts toward conserving our natural resources.

By making the deletions I've suggested in your long letter, which I assume you sent to a lot of people in addition to me, you would have been able to get your message all on one page. This would have produced a 100 percent saving in paper for every letter you sent and saved at least the limb of a good-sized tree.

Peter E. Overton
Olympia, Washington

Dear Mr. Overton,

Call me "uninformed and short-sighted" but many of the arguments I hear from different people in the tree business sound like doubletalk carefully orchestrated by public relations people, expert at the business of deflecting criticism.

The use of such terms as "tree farmer," "forest management," "family forestry" and "processed forest products" is designed to flimflam the public. I buy boards but please, don't tell me it's good for the forest. To say "more trees are growing today than seventy years ago" is being deliberately deceptive. Are there more board feet growing today than seventy years ago? How old are you? You're a tree "farmer?" Has your company ever "harvested" a tree that was planted since you came into the business? How many of the redwoods cut last year developed to their size in your lifetime? It is true to suggest, as lumber companies always do, that "trees are a renewable resource." So is coal I suppose but most of the great trees we have cut down and most of the coal we've dug will never be "renewed."

You say "Log exports allow for intensive forest management . . . ." What does that mean? Why would log exports allow for any different forest management than lumber export which would provide jobs for American lumber mill workers?

John Walburn, MD
Creighton Univ School of Medicine
Omaha, Nebraska

Dear Dr. Walburn,

It's good to hear of a professional who has encouraging things to say about any part of our welfare system.

Those of us who live in New York see welfare in a different light. You say there's evidence that in Nebraska "welfare is generally a short-term assist through hard times." As you must know, it is nothing like that in New York. There are often three generations in a family that has never lived on anything but welfare and ending the arrangement is not a thought that comes to their minds.

I've always thought of myself as a social and political liberal but I suppose my opinions, like my arteries, are hardening.

. . .

James Bowling
Senior Vice President
Philip Morris

Dear Jim,

Thank you for pointing out my mistake in saying that Philip Morris earnings in other areas of its business exceeded those for tobacco.

There's no doubt that you are the cigarette industry's foremost apologist. You do the job with skill and grace. Your temperate letter to me is a good example. I appreciate seeing anyone do anything well in the world where things are being done so badly; all I wish is that you were devoting your ability toward a better cause. The thought of quitting Philip Morris must have crossed your mind.

I'm thoroughly familiar with the potential for logical fallacy in medical statistics but the only alternative to the conclusion that cigarette smoking causes lung cancer is that people who are congenitally destined to develop lung cancer have an urge from youth to smoke cigarettes. If the first contention has not been proved beyond the shadow of a scientific doubt because of the continuing mystery of the actual nature of cancer, the second seems highly improbable.

Hope to see you and Ann soon.

Ron Jette
L'Association Pulmonaire
Gloucester, Ontario

Dear Mr. Jette,

There's nothing in your letter I disagree with except your belief that it's a good idea to try to eliminate cigarette smoking by taxing them beyond anyone's desire or ability to pay to buy them. That's not a grownup way to attack the problem.

It's been proven that beef produces cholesterol in the body's plumbing system. Would you make taxes prohibitively high on meat? What about automobile accident deaths? Quadruple the sales tax on cars? Close highways? How about assessing everything we consume in relation to its effect on our life expectancy and taxing it accordingly?

I haven't thought of it since college but your statement about the decline of cigarette smoking in Canada following the imposition of heavy taxes was known in logic class then as a "post hoc ergo propter hoc" fallacy.

Maybe Canadians stopped smoking, not because of the tax but because they got smarter.

. . .

It is always a surprise to find yourself being quoted as having said something nothing like what you said.

Mr. Richard J. Pamperin
President
Marion State Bank
Marion, Wisconsin

Dear Mr. Pamperin,

It was not clear from your letter of December 2nd whether you were being ignorant or devious.

You quoted me about farmers as having said "they are an honest, independent, hardworking bunch. Little by little, though, farmers are becoming less admired than they once were. None of them really work."

If you have passed that on as a quotation from me in writing to anyone else, I would look into legal action against you.

You took one sentence "They were an honest, independent, hardworking bunch" and then dropped the next sentence in my column "More than any other single group, they have made this country what it is, great."

Then you took one sentence from the next paragraph "Little by little, though, farmers are becoming less admired than they once were" and, in an unbelievable job of distorting what I said, jumped fourteen paragraphs and dropped in the sentence "None of them really work."

In my text that sentence referred to the one in front of it, which read "The Government has come up with all sorts of devious plans. None of them really work." "None of them work" clearly referred to Government plans, not to farmers. Is this the way you keep your books at the Marion State Bank?

I would like an apology.

To Mr. Pamperin's credit, he wrote to apologize.

. . .

Bobby L. Dexter
Harvard Law School

Dear Mr., or possibly Ms., Dexter,

I trust you'll be flattered to hear that I've posted your letter, addressed to me care of *20/20*, ABC on the *60 Minutes* bulletin board here at CBS as evidence of what we can expect from future Harvard Law School graduates.

I made some negative comments about Arabic and other Middle Eastern languages and the virtues of English.

Dave Mathews
Houston, Texas

Dear Dave,

I don't know what gets into me but even though I'm basically a liberal, I am amused at being hardhat once in a while. You know . . . I thought we were right involving ourselves in the war in the Middle East, I'm ambivalent about abortion and I think everyone in the United States should speak English. Things like that.

Arabic is one of the things that holds back Middle Eastern countries. They have typewriters and computers, as you say, but the typewriters are unwieldy and impractical.

You don't have to be a chauvinist to think that English is the best language. It is dominant in the world, not because we are dominant economically, militarily and culturally, but because it's a better language than Japanese, French, German or Spanish and certainly better as a communications tool than Arabic.

The great language expert, Mario Pei, once wrote down for me a short paragraph in English and then proceeded to translate it into French, German, Spanish and finally Vietnamese. It got longer and longer because the shortage of words in many languages calls for lengthy circumlocutions to get across the same idea than can be expressed briefly in English.

I enjoyed getting your letter. It's not often I'm accused of being chauvinistic by a Texan.

Becky Speraw
New Albany, Ohio

Dear Ms. Speraw,

It seems probable that I should not have put my comments about Gov. Celeste's release of the women who murdered their husbands, in so flip a column.

Having conceded you that much, I'm not willing to go farther. Murder is against the law. It's that simple. The law is not sentimental. If you think murder is okay under certain circumstances, you're suggesting a new law that would be impossible to write.

Giving me details of cases in which women have been abused was an illogical way to argue your case. My wife taught in the school where Jean Harris was headmistress and after Jean murdered Tarnhower, her supporters said he was a bad guy—as though that made the murder excusable.

I've never seen a convicted murderer I couldn't feel sorry for. Each has a story. In civilized countries, murder is illegal no matter how nice the murderer is or how evil the victim was.

. . .

A thousand times a year, I am approached by someone doing good work for a legitimate cause that needs help.

Arthur Goodfriend was assigned to The Stars and Stripes *as a major late during WW II. He was charming and capable but infuriated other staff members because he was an incurable propagandist. He wrote some heavy-handed editorials that were run over the protest of the newspaper's editors.*

He continued his good works into his nineties. I turned down his request for help ten times and never got over feeling guilty about it.

Arthur Goodfriend
Alzheimer's Association
Honolulu, Hawaii

Dear Arthur,

Your Alzheimer's brochure is beautifully done and I should think might be effective in achieving the end you hope for.

I am surprised though that you'd think I would get into the kind of a promotional stunt you outline even for so deserving a cause as your Alzheimer's crusade. You know what I do. The most certain way a writer can kill any hope he ever has of doing something good is to become a propagandist of any kind.

It may make me sound uncaring to you but I do not take on good causes no matter how good the causes are. Yours sounds like one of the best but I don't do *60 Minutes* pieces about dangerous toys, blindness, deafness, AIDS, cancer, battered women, drunk driving or SIDS although sincere and good people working in these areas approach me regularly. It isn't that I don't feel like helping. It's that I know that destroying my credibility is not the way for me to help.

Keep up your good work and I'll try to keep up mine—different though it is from yours. I was pleased to see, noting the excellence of your brochure, that you don't seem to have lost a step. You still know how to do it.

. . .

Hamilton Davis, inevitably known to his classmates as "Ham," was a big tall, red-headed end on the football team, Phi Beta Kappa and president of our class at Colgate. Ham became an outstanding anesthesiologist at the University of

California, Davis. Because his name and the location of the medical school where he taught were the same, I always thought he should have changed one of them.

In 1981 he wrote imploring me to try to help do something about gun control by publicizing the issues and by lending my name to an organization promoting it. I repeat, he wrote me in 1981.

"Having observed the mayhem in our emergency room for many years" he wrote, "I'm convinced that something has to be done to start to disarm our Country. I doubt that legislators are going to act—they never have."

Dear Ham,

It's always a bad idea for a journalist to espouse a cause but if I was going to espouse one, it would be gun control. Your relatively modest approach "to start to disarm this Country" is a good one to take.

I can't get over how modest all the proposals are for gun control. A congressman will put up a bill making it mandatory for someone to wait twenty minutes before he can take possession of a weapon in a gun store and it will be defeated as being too restrictive and unAmerican.

There was a recent proposal for a law stating that a person could not buy a gun more than once every thirty days, I think it was. That means a law-abiding citizen could only buy twelve guns a year. I wondered at the time how many guns a law-abiding citizen would want to buy if there were *no* limit.

All Al Capone would have to do today if he wanted to buy a sawed off shotgun or an AK-47 would be to go to a gun show.

I'm enthusiastic about your crusade but I'm not going to join it.

You will be pleased to know that the proselytizing you did on behalf of California wines when we saw you and Marge, has had some effect on my drinking custom although I am such an infrequent wine-drinker that I doubt that the industry will detect any great upswing in sales as a result of it.

Love to Marge and regards to you,

. . .

In 1981 it amused me one day to look at pictures of a lot of old Miss America contestants and choose some I thought were something less than beauties.

One of the girls I picked to show was the 1942 winner, Jo-Carroll Dennison.

A few days later, I got a letter from Phil Silvers, who established himself in the 1950s as one of television's greatest all-time comedians in his role as Sergeant Bilko, written by Nat Hiken.

I never met Phil but the pathetic letter he wrote made me feel terrible. "Your snide reference to an ex Miss America of the early 1940s touched a nerve. Her name was Jo-Carroll Dennison and at the illegal age of 17, she won every event in the Pageant. She was signed as an actress to 20th Century Fox where we met and were married."

Dear Phil,

I always feel badly when my attempt at humor hurts someone. Originally I had planned to pick the homeliest Miss America there has ever been but realized that was too cruel to do to anyone.

My only defense of poking fun at those old winners is that, to some extent, I think the girls make themselves fair game for ridicule when they enter a contest like that. The picture of Jo-Carroll Dennison was overly dramatic and funny for that reason but my comment was not really very mean to her.

Anyway, I apologize. Had I known what you told me, I would not have done it.

Brad Wilks
Ball Corporation
Muncie, Indiana

Dear Mr. Wilks,

Of course I'm sorry if I was in error with my comment about the demise of Ball Jars. That's what I thought I read in my newspaper. The problem is that people, including journalists, don't understand the grammatical nuances of corporate English.

You might have anticipated trouble from them when your initial press release began by saying:

"Ball Corporation (NYSE:BBL) today said its board of directors had approved, in principle, the spin-off to Ball shareholders of the stock of a newly formed subsidiary consisting of certain operations outside of the company's core businesses of glass and metal packaging, and aerospace." and ended by saying ". . . the business units which are the subject of the spin-off will be classified as a discontinued business in Ball's future financial reporting."

See—this sounds fatal to someone who doesn't understand corporate talk. I'm sorry if my translation was in error.

Eleanor Lansdowne
New York, New York

Dear Miss Lansdowne,

I'm sorry I disappointed you but I think royalty is nonsense. The British would be better off without it.

Nothing that happens to these people has any effect whatsoever on our lives so Americans can view these distant events with detached amusement. Of course it doesn't make any difference in England, either, but the British don't seem to understand that and they don't understand how ridiculous the idea of a royal family seems to us.

Charles and Di were both caught fooling around with someone other than each other and it made great reading for the British people and for those Americans who follow them as a hobby but it doesn't have anything to do with the real world. If it amuses the British people to make a continuing soap opera out of their royal family, I don't care but they should know that it makes them look foolish in the eyes of the world.

. . .

Diane Bennett
American Diabetes Association
Fort Myers, Florida

Dear Ms. Bennett,

It is almost always a mistake to write a letter of complaint based on what someone else told you they thought they heard me say.

PART TEN

Judging Lawyers

When I wrote about lawyers who work on a contingency basis, I got a hundred angry letters—all from lawyers. One was from a college classmate practicing law in California who doesn't work on contingency but resented what I said anyway.

Dear Ralph,

It was good to hear from you after all these years, even with a complaint. You said you've liked a lot of things I've done. So, how come you waited to write until I did something you disliked?

I wasn't condemning lawyers, I was condemning bad lawyers and also condemning good lawyers for not doing something about bad lawyers. Good lawyers are the only ones who can do anything because you're the only ones who know whether one of your professional brothers is honest or dishonest, ethical or unethical.

You guys ought to be angrier than anyone at the soft or rotten apples in your barrel because they make all of you look bad and that's not right.

I know all the arguments in favor of contingency fees—poor people would never be represented if lawyers didn't have a chance to make a lot of money on the cases they win. Insurance companies would get away with murder and manufacturers would never be held to any safety standards. If I admit there's a case to be made for the contingency system you have to admit that it tends to attract the sleazebag lawyers. You must have looked at the ads in the yellow pages of the L.A. phone book under LAWYERS.

I'm glad I'm not a lawyer because it would be too hard to decide some of the ethical questions involved in practicing law. Like, for example, do you take a client you think is guilty and defend him because that's your business?

I ran across a dialog between Samuel Johnson and Boswell.

I thought was great even though it's on your side of the argument. Feel free to use it in your defense of lawyers:

Boswell: (questioning Johnson about lawyers): What do you think of supporting a cause that you know to be bad?

Johnson: Sir, you do not know it to be good or bad until the judge determines it . . . an argument that does not convince yourself, may convince the Judge to whom you urge it, and, if it does convince him, why, then, Sir, you are wrong and he is right.

Boswell: But, Sir, does not affecting a warmth when you have no warmth and appearing to be clearly of one opinion when you are of another . . . impair a lawyer's honesty? Is there not some danger that a lawyer may put on the same mask . . . with his friends?

Johnson: Why, no, Sir. Everybody knows you are paid for affecting warmth for your client . . . the moment you come from the bar, you resume your usual behavior. A man will no more carry the artifice of the bar into common society than a man who is paid for tumbling upon his hands will continue to tumble on his hands when he can walk on his feet."

But I don't know why I'm giving you ammunition. Lawyers already have the upper hand.

Bruce Preston
Adams & Knox
Cincinnati, Ohio

Dear Mr. Preston,

First let me give you a little non legal advice: When you write a dumb, personal letter don't put it on the stationery of the law firm you work for.

My second bit of advice *is* legal: Don't quote me as having said something I didn't say, and can prove I didn't say by producing the tape, or you could need a lawyer yourself.

My last bit of advice is easy: If you're going to use his name in a letter, learn how to spell Stephen Sondheim's name.

. . .

Benjamin Kelley
Institute for Injury Reduction
Defense Highway
Crofton, Maryland

Dear Mr. Kelley,

You have always impressed me as being an articulate spokesman for your organization but I remain skeptical of the motives of the Institute for Injury Reduction.

In offering your list of corrections to my statements, you start by quoting me as saying something I didn't say and follow that up with a question you don't answer. I quite clearly did not say your organization was supported by the American Trial Lawyers Association. I did say it was supported by "many members of ATLA." Any correction called for there?

Second point: You ask ". . . does that not lead to fewer rather than more lawsuits?" What's the answer, do you know? Are there any statistics on the diminishing number of lawsuits? If there are fewer lawsuits in this area in the past ten or twenty years, it would be a news story. Please send me any figures you have that supports your statement.

How many members do you have? You say you have "a handful (200 or so)" lawyers, "Some of them ATLA members." Is 200 really a very small part, a "handful" of your membership? Could you send me a list of your members? Because you are a charitable organization soliciting contributions from the public, I believe it should be made available.

I think, as I said on the air, that the Institute has had a salutary effect on the toy industry but I also think the problem has been overstated. If your organization was devoted to pedestrian safety, no kid would ever cross the street because so many of them are killed doing it every year. It's a big Country and bad things happen no matter what it is a lot of people do.

I was amused by your statement that "[lawyers] get substantial fees if they win, and nothing . . . if they lose." You must be familiar with the story of the lawyer who told his client "If I don't win this case, I get absolutely nothing. If I win this case, YOU get absolutely nothing."

I said trial lawyers had spoiled a lot of things. The makers of ladders spend more on insurance against people who sue them when they fall off one than they spend on making their ladders in the first place. I said it was difficult to buy a springboard. One lawyer wrote a long letter saying, among other things, that it wasn't true about springboards . . . that I could get one right near his hometown if I wanted to. I followed up on it because I did want to buy one.

Peter N. Munsing
Wyomissing, Pennsylvania

Dear Mr. Munsing,

Today I called Sylvan Pool Supplies which you said you found as "a supplier for a springboard."

A transcript of my conversation with the woman who answered the phone went like this:

> ME: Do you have springboards in stock?
> S.P.S.: No we do not.
> ME: Can I buy a springboard from you?
> S.P.: Is it for a Sylvan pool that we installed?
> ME: No. It's for a dock on a lake.
> S.P.: We only sell replacement diving boards to Sylvan Pool owners because of the litigation aspect.

Reread your letter in which you assured me I could buy one.

Larry S. Stewart
President
Association of Trial Lawyers of America
Miami, Florida

Dear Mr. Stewart,

It must be difficult for you to believe but yes, I do think the Association of Trial Lawyers has an ulterior motive in being the principal supporter of the Institute for Injury Reduction and its annual campaign to make the public aware of how dangerous toys are.

Faulty thinking of this kind by people like me points up how much work your organization has to do to improve the public's perception of trial lawyers. My crazy, wild suggestion, as a means of accomplishing this public relations transformation, would be for the legal profession to rid itself of the sleazy, unethical element in its midst. Or would that be out of the question?

PART ELEVEN

Hard Hobbies

Marc James Small
Roanoke, Virginia

Dear Mr. Small,

From now on, when I think of Rush Limbaugh listeners, I'll think of you as an exception.

As a football fan myself, I disagree with you that the game appeals to "feeble-minded seekers of vicarious thrills." We aren't necessarily feeble-minded although I concede that while we're watching, we set aside any real brains we have. See, that's the beauty of it. We get all excited about this event that doesn't have a damn thing to do with real life. No matter what happens, it doesn't really matter. It's a mini-vacation.

You say you don't watch television. Well, I get as much pleasure watching a football game as you get from not watching television. People who don't watch television are as proud of themselves as football fans are proud of their team. A non-watcher of television never misses a chance to announce that he is superior to both television and the people who do watch it. We all need to feel superior to something or someone and I've chosen to feel superior to Rush Limbaugh and the Washington Redskins.

Marv Levy
Buffalo, New York

Dear Marv,

It was good of you to write. No one gets tired of praise.

Years ago I was in a crowd with Diane Sawyer. People kept coming up to her and telling her how beautiful she looked. In a quiet moment I asked her if it wasn't a pain in the neck having people tell her how beautiful she is all the time. She paused a moment and said, "Well . . . actually I have quite a high tolerance for that sort of thing."

I like football and the good people in the game. You're one of them. I played briefly for Andy Kerr at Colgate in 1940 and '41—he was one of them. Fred Swan was line coach. He wasn't one. Fred was caught up with stunting—making the game complex for linemen. It was brand new then.

Good luck next year although I don't put much stock in luck. I'll be rooting for you and the Bills right up to the day you play the Giants.

Mark Murphy
Athletic Director
Colgate University
Hamilton, New York

Dear Mark,

It might be easier to be President of the United States than to do the job you're undertaking as athletic director.

I would be more inclined to support the Colgate Athletic Council if I weren't suspicious of it. An Alumni group supporting a football team outside a college's regular bookkeeping system has created trouble wherever one has existed.

We tread the ragged edge of all the evils that afflict college sports at Colgate and I would not like to see us go the way of so many colleges that have made a business of a game. I'm not even thinking of such monstrous, anti-educational programs as those at such places as the various Floridas.

Colgate's close win over Columbia this year was exactly where we should be. If we play in our own league and win more than half our games over a ten year period, we're probably cheating. That's true of any college. Every once in a while we should win all of them, of course. And then, every once in a while we should *lose* all of them if we play the game honestly.

Colgate owes much of its reputation as an educational institution to the football teams of the late 1930s. We became better known than a small college would normally have been because we played with, and often beat, the big time football teams in the Country. It's ironic that Colgate is now a vastly better academic institution with higher standards than it was when its football team was unbeaten because those football teams attracted the large numbers of applicants that allowed Colgate to be more selective.

I know how alumni giving at a college is directly reflected by the success or failure of the football team. I nonetheless hope we—you—can resist the temptation to use the tactics and the money that the semi-pro colleges use in recruiting and attracting football players. I hope Colgate can live by the standards of the schools in its educational class. Ivy League schools seem to be handling it pretty well. Most of the guys on the team can spell.

Howard Stringer, a former president of CBS, now president of Sony, America, is one of my most successful old friends.

Howard,

Thanks for getting Virginia to arrange for the Super Bowl ticket. Much appreciated and I had a great time.

I bought a video camera and tried to make a home movie of my trip to the game for *60 Minutes*. I shot a lot of different stuff and some of it was pretty good.

Walking along the main street in Atlanta, camera at the ready, I saw Bob Tisch coming out of Woolworth's. The line I wrote over the picture of him emerging from the Five and Ten, is "I saw my friend Bob Tisch in Atlanta. Bob owns half of the New York Giants and he's one of the richest men in America. He was coming out of Woolworth's. I don't know what Bob was buying in Woolworth's—Woolworth's maybe."

After your graceful remarks at the event last night, I saw Larry Tisch. We're going to use the picture of his brother in our *60 Minutes* piece, and in an effort to make sure he knew I was doing it in the spirit of good fun, I told Larry about my line about Brother Bob buying Woolworth's.

Larry just looked at me, not unfriendly but not smiling, and he said, in all seriousness "No. No one would buy Woolworth's now . . . the condition the company's in."

Pat Harmon is on the board of the College Football Hall of Fame and writes me regularly. He's always thinking about which former college players should be admitted.

Dear Pat,

Yes, I know of Winnie Anderson. When I was at The Albany Academy we booked a game with Manlius, a military prep school that some of the big football colleges used to store players while they got a year older. Their team was normally out of our league but one year our coach thought we had a strong team and booked Manlius.

Winnie Anderson was their coach.

The game was played at night in Hawkins Stadium in Albany in front of 10,000 people. The Manlius team came out to warm up wearing white jerseys with maroon stripes on their sleeves. Three squads ran up and down the field and we couldn't help sneaking a peak. It looked as if they were running plays without a football.

When it was time for the kickoff, Winnie Anderson came out with a football painted white with maroon stripes that exactly matched the markings on the sleeves of the Manlius jerseys. When one of their players held a ball in his arm, it was all but invisible.

There was a 15 minute delay of the kickoff while our coach, Bill Morris, refused to send us out if the striped balls were used. Winnie Anderson claimed the visiting team had the right to choose the game balls. The referee finally decided in our favor and we played with a regular, pigskin-colored ball.

The game ended in a scoreless tie and it was the greatest victory our undefeated team had that year.

Ms. Elisabeth Muhlenfeld
Division of Undergraduate Studies
The Florida State University

Dear Dean Muhlenfeld,

Thank you for your informative letter.

I'm sorry if I've maligned the academic record of your football team. I was aware that Charlie Ward was considered a good student.

If you can send me a list of the courses being taken by the starters on the 1993 team, their 1992 grades and their SAT averages submitted for admission to FSU, it is quite possible that I can make a correction.

It would also be helpful if I could have the graduation record of last year's senior starters.

I look forward to your reply.

There was no reply.

. . .

John Mercer
New Orleans, Louisiana

Dear John,

Your eggnog letter fell on hearing ears. It often seems as though the direction everything in the whole world takes is always away from quality. They find a way to replace a genuine ingredient with something artificial that's cheaper and doesn't taste as good. "Just like butter" they say.

I dislike the whole idea of store-bought eggnog. I think they use artificial nog and imitation eggs. Part of the fun of eggnog is making it.

We have a party for sixty people at New Years. My recipe varies but it is something like this:

Fifth Myers dark rum, fifth bourbon, fifth cheap cognac, four quarts heavy cream, a lot of sugar, (keep tasting), two dozen eggs, separated—whites beaten and added to mixture just before serving from cut glass bowl left to you by your wife's mother. Provide grater with little dish of whole nutmegs for people to sprinkle over top themselves.

I warn people that this is not a toy drink to be consumed as though it was dessert.

It may disturb a scientist to hear but I keep leftover eggnog in the refrigerator and use it as a mellow starter the following year. It thickens. No ill friends over past thirty-five years.

. . .

Al Durante
Forest Hills Garden
New York, New York

Dear Al,

Yes, of course I remember you. I was looking for you when I wrote that column about bourbon. There are still four or five good bourbons and four or five that aren't very good. The worst is the biggest seller, isn't that the American way?

The bourbon industry hasn't done anywhere near what the Scotch distillers have done in giving its drink a cachet. Americans don't know what a good, all-American drink bourbon is and they don't understand that every bottle of bourbon is comparable to a single malt Scotch. It is unadulterated with neutral grain spirits.

I drink and enjoy it but it's difficult to defend even with the recent medical evidence suggesting that a couple of drinks a day may be good for what ails you if it's your heart that's ailing. Young people are drinking less and they're probably right—unless they substitute marijuana or something stronger for alcohol.

I resent the bad name drinking has taken on over the years though because of a small number of people who drink, drive and kill themselves or someone else. I think of the kind of drinking we do, two before dinner while we watch the news, as a civilized little ceremony at the end of the working day. If my mind is slightly altered by it, it's for the better.

. . .

Dear Ed,

As much as I love ice cream and enjoyed reading your publication, *The Ice Screamer*, I don't think I'll join your group. I already belong to as many groups as I have time to meet with and get as many publications as I can throw away without reading.

My point was to convince people of how simple it is to make ice cream. Like bread, all the cookbooks make it more complicated than it is. This is how to make ice cream:

Mix together a quart of milk with as much cream as you can afford, a cup of sugar and a few spoonfuls of vanilla. Freeze it. Don't cook anything. If you want frozen custard, not ice cream, use eggs and cook the mixture before you freeze it the way they tell you to do it in all the cookbooks.

We started making ice cream in the summer as kids at the Lake. Before electric refrigerators, everyone had an ice man who came every other day to put a new cake in the ice box. We'd get the ice man to drop an extra twenty-five pound block for us. There were four kids and we took turns churning the White Mountain freezer. One summer, the smart one among us, Buster Scovill, devised an attachment with an electric motor that turned the paddles inside the freezer for us. I suppose someone had a patent for an electric ice cream freezer before Buster made that when he was seventeen but his was ahead of any electric freezer I saw for twenty years.

Now I make peach, coffee, strawberry, raspberry, orange-lemon, chocolate. Chocolate's hardest to make well. You can make ice cream with two cups of maple syrup.

I'm surprised how good the best brands of commercial ice cream are. It diminishes my enthusiasm for making it myself.

Dr. Brewer
University of California at Davis

Dr. Brewer,

In your October letter to me, you said "Several decades ago the tomato was thought to be poisonous."

Well, several years ago, the tomato was thought to be round, red and tasty too. That's before your colleagues in California, with grants from the spaghetti sauce people, developed a tomato that was square, light pink, hard and tasteless—but was cheap and easy to pick and pack with machinery.

When you told me about pears, you were still talking about shipping them not eating them. I know you can't ship a ripe pear. You can ship a pear that isn't ripe but when it gets where it's going, you can't eat it. Which is better?

I appreciated your letter but I want to be absolutely honest . . . I'm suspicious of anyone called an "Agricultural Economist." Like "military music," it's a contradiction in terms.

An importer of some gourmet food items from Ireland, sent me several tins of McCann's Irish Oatmeal, which I like.

It's the real grain "steel cut" into small, hard kernels.

Assuming my heritage, he included some remarks about his pride in being Irish.

Dear Jack,

I've never spent much time being Irish. I'm proud of it and pride has always been a motivating force in the world but I'm turned off by too much of it. It's only good, it seems to me, in limited amounts. I even question whether, in the long run, patriotism has been a force for good or evil in the world. The Nazis were proud of being German. I don't distinguish "nationalism" with "patriotism." Take a look at what patriotism is doing on the borders of countries of the world today. Patriotism and religion are the two principal reasons that the people of one country set out to kill the people of another.

We spent a pleasant ten days in Ireland several years ago in the company of Harry Reasoner, his wife, Kay and Dermot Doran, a priest who works with Catholic Relief Services. Dermot's brother has a pub on Third Avenue and his mother runs one just outside Dublin.

Kay Reasoner is Catholic and always called Dermot "Father Doran." The rest of us called him "Dermot." He was fun to be with and, when we were on our way to Dublin, we asked Dermot if his mother called him "Father."

We're enjoying the McCann's Irish Oatmeal you sent although I'm thinking of writing McCann's to suggest they redo their directions for cooking it. It's strange how often a company doesn't know how to prepare its own product. McCann's recommends using almost four times as much water as is needed and recommends cooking it more than twice as long as is good for oatmeal unless you want gruel.

Ironically, the last line under the instructions reads "To ensure characteristic rich nutty flavor, avoid overcooking."

They say to cook a cup of oatmeal in four cups of water for half an hour. Wrong! I cook a cup of real oatmeal in a cup and a half of water and salt. Bring it to a boil, turn it low for three or four minutes, then turn it off and let it sit for ten or fifteen minutes more.

How can a company whose livelihood depends on people liking their product, put such bad information about how to fix it, on its label?

Real oatmeal is so much better than the instant flakes or processed, sugar-laden cereal most people buy that I think it would catch on, in a limited way, as a breakfast food in this Country but it needs a little promotion and a decent recipe on the can. I say "in a limited way" because I know a lot of Americans won't take the time to cook it. They're the same Americans who eat TV dinners.

. . .

Edward E. Wallach, M.D.
Baltimore, Maryland

Dear Dr. Wallach,

Yes, the desk you see on television is one I made.

I regret not having visited George Nakashima's woodworking shop in New Hope before he died. Six weeks ago we finally drove there and had an interesting few hours looking around. One of his daughters has taken over production of new pieces which are nice but the genius is gone.

My shop is in a small town in upstate New York. I have good tools and more interesting pieces of wood than I have years left to make anything of but I love just having the wood to look at and touch every day.

My desk is made from a walnut flitch I bought from a tree surgeon named Willard near Trenton. The Willard Brothers are unusual in that they make boards out of any good tree that has come down or that they've had to take down. Most tree surgeons butcher good logs, cutting them into fireplace length. It breaks my heart to see. Someone in our town cut down a cherry tree 23" in diameter and chopped it up. I tried to make them feel bad by telling them it would have been worth $15,000 if it had been milled into boards.

The dovetails in my desk are ebony. Pure Nakishima. I no longer look at a split in a heavy board as a defect. The two upright supports, the legs of my desk, are made from a walnut bar taken from an old hotel they demolished near us.

I'm not a great cabinetmaker but I use good wood and good tools. People are so surprised that I can do it at all that they don't notice my shortcomings.

. . .

Julius H. Vince
Fairfield, Connecticut

Dear Mr. Vince,

You've assumed by now that I ignored your good letter but I didn't. I put it in a special pile that I want to make sure I answer and I didn't answer those, either.

I am, at the moment of writing, in a small, five-sided structure I built five years ago to write in when we are at our summer place here thirty miles southwest of Albany. My little pentagon is a perfect place to write because there are no windows except the five, triangular ones in each of the roof panels. Each of the five sides of the building is eight-feet long.

My beloved pentagon is 100 feet from the kitchen in the main house and twenty feet from the door of my woodworking shop so it's easy for me to stop working and either eat or saw wood.

. . .

Edwin L. Bass
Jersey City, New Jersey

Dear Mr. Bass,

I've been in the showroom of your store on Lafayette Street many times. I bought my Makita 15¾ inch thickness planer from you.

My workshop is filled with tools. Some of them are good and I use them frequently; others are poor and I wonder why I bought them because I never use them. I wish I knew in advance which was going to be which. It's like the clothes in your closet. You have to own them for a few months before you know for sure whether or not you should have bought them.

My planer would be even better if I hadn't spent all one day installing new carbide blades and shortly thereafter run a very old wide pine board through it and hit an ancient nail I'd failed to extract. It nicked the blade so every time I put a board through it, there's one tiny ridge the length of it where the nick is. Someone told me that if I loosened one of the blades and tapped it on the side with a hammer, it would change the position of the two blades so that the nicks were not in line.

I have most of what I need, a good Powermatic tablesaw and long bed planer, a big Makita band saw (resaw) which is hard and dangerous to use, a Delta bandsaw, an el cheapo drill press from Taiwan, a Delta combination disc/belt sander and a Sears lathe which is barely fair.

Then I have all the hand tools, many of them twice. I admire the cabinetmakers who prefer doing things by hand but I'm not one of them.

I've bought most of my tools from a grand old Albany hardware store there, R.B. Wing & Sons. They have hardware no one will ever buy if they stay in business another 100 years. That's what a hardware store ought to have. The owner, Tod Wing, won't sell Japanese tools so I get those from a more modern tool store nearby.

I have a great collection of wood. Lots of 25" wide cherry 14' long, some very good heavy walnut and a selection of curly and birdseye maple. I also have several varieties of mahogany, teak, rosewood, coca bola and macassar ebony but in the past few years I've turned away from the exotic stuff. I prefer the native American wood if the furniture is going to be used in America. I have some nice figured apple boards that are full of knots and are short. Apple trees don't grow tall but it's beautiful wood with all its flaws. I've made some nice pieces with it and I'm always looking for more.

Tod Wing's Hardware didn't stay in business. Like thousands of good, local hardware stores, it was driven out by the giants.

PART TWELVE

Home Sweet-and-Sour Home

Janice Auld
Miami, Florida

Dear Janice,

It was good to get your letter about Evans's Grocery Store. The store was important in my young life and I remember absolutely everything about it.

Your great grandfather, who started the store and Frank, your grandfather, were an unlikely father and son team. Frank was tall, or seemed tall to me at the time, and grumpy. His father was short and, generally, better-natured. Neither of them was good-natured but I liked them both.

Even though I was quite young—I suppose I went to the store between the ages of seven and twelve—they kidded me a lot and I believe, although I'm not sure, that I kidded them. I don't know whether you kid anyone when you're seven or not.

The customers didn't pick what they wanted in a grocery store in those days. They told the man behind the counter what they wanted and he went and got it for them. There was no browsing and walking up and down the aisles with a cart or a basket.

Evans's store was small so a lot of the food was on shelves that went from floor to ceiling. Customers didn't go behind the counter. The shelves were so high that, in some cases, Frank had to use a pair of those pincers on the end of a six foot stick to take down a box or a can of something the customer wanted. There was a hook on the back of the stick, behind the pincers and if it was a box of cereal you wanted, Frank would tip the box with the hook until it fell off the shelf and then he'd catch it.

Just a few grocery store items are the same now as they were then. Shredded Wheat looks the same. Heinz Catsup or Ketchup, Gulden's Mustard, Crisco, Lorna Doone, Fig Newton cookies.

In the summer they kept a display of fruits and vegetables under an awning over the front of the store.

The ice box with meat, butter, milk and eggs was in a small area at the back of the store. It was not a refrigerator, it was an insulated closet about twelve feet long and seven feet high with several hundred-pound blocks of ice in it to keep everything cool. Your grandfather watched anyone who went back there like a hawk and if the person left the ice-box door open for more than the time it took to grab something, he'd yell at them to close it.

I suspect part of what made them grumpy was that business wasn't very good during the Depression. Everyone charged things and some people didn't pay their bills. When your great grandfather wouldn't give them anymore credit, they'd just go to the other grocery store halfway down Madison Avenue on the other side of the street, Flynn's, and start charging food there.

Both your great grandfather and your grandfather liked us as customers because we were able to pay our grocery bill. Mr. Evans always gave me a Baby Ruth, an Oh Henry or a Tootsie Roll when I brought the check my mother had given me to pay the bill with.

We knew something funny was going on between Sarah, the cashier, and your father. Sure enough, after your mother died, Frank and Sarah got married. Sarah was the best-natured one in the store. She had a good personality and helped keep the two Franks from being rude to the customers.

To get to Evans's on Madison Avenue from our house on Partridge Street, I took the shortcut behind the Baptist church on the corner.

Some crazy got into the church one night and destroyed much of the interior of it, breaking up the pulpit and turning the pews upside down.

I recall taking the shortcut that day and seeing a three-legged piano stool that he had tried to throw through the stained glass window picturing Christ in a pasture with three lambs. The stool got stuck halfway through the heavy window, held there by the leaded dividers between the sections of colored glass.

On the way home with the groceries, I didn't take the shortcut behind the church. It was too spooky. I stayed out on the street.

You can see that I enjoyed being reminded of Evans's grocery store. Thank you.

Dear Mr. Emmerling,

Arnold Mayersohn lives in Little Rock and I went to The Academy with him so I know that it's possible to migrate from Albany to Little Rock as you did.

There are just a few things I think of to say about your letter:

An uncle of mine, Herbert Prescott, was editor of The Albany Argus although I don't know during what period. I delivered *The Knickerbocker Press* after school.

The houses on Manning Boulevard you spoke of were set back from the road. They were widely separated and usually had about seven steps up to the porch so it was hard to deliver papers to them. I can't imagine what the economics of the newspaper business was . . . The "*Knick*" cost five cents and I got a penny for delivering one. My route had thirty-seven houses.

I folded the papers into eight-inch squares so I could throw them onto a porch without having to climb the steps but I often missed.

When they went into the bushes, I had to go get them. I'm not clear whether those were the houses to which you delivered or not.

We go into Albany occasionally. The houses on Manning Boulevard are not nearly so grand or far apart as I recall them.

The area noted as "St. Mary's Park" on plate II of the pictures you sent was known to us as Orphan Asylum Hill because it was adjacent to what we called "the Orphan Asylum." You wouldn't call it that anymore. We used the hill for sledding when there was snow and the lower, flat part for playing football Saturday mornings.

Western Avenue was paved with cobblestone and it must have been tough on car chains because I recall the sound of broken chains slapping against the under side of the fenders of old Fords and Chevvies.

Hageman's Bakery (not Hagerman's) was on Madison Avenue and made good New Year's cookies but otherwise not much anyone would consider gourmet. They set the standard for bad lemon custard pies with soggy cardboard crusts, which my father loved.

An eight-story building was put up kittycorner from the high school on Western Avenue called The Eloise Apartments. My cousins, Herb and Jack Prescott, made a parachute out of old bedsheets and were caught on top of the building just as Herb was about to jump and see if the parachute worked—which it would not have.

In comic strips, I liked "Buck Rogers" and his girlfriend "Wilma" but one of the first news stories I recall reading may have been during your years there. It was when Mayor Hackett was killed in some kind of a car accident—falling out of one I think it was—in Florida.

If you don't have it, you ought to buy my friend William Kennedy's book *O Albany!* Every city should have a novelist of its own like Bill. He's the Pulitzer Prize-winning author of *Legs* and *Ironweed*, both set in Albany.

When you deal with a contractor, you have to decide in advance that things will probably not work out the way you thought they would and you're going to have to pay anyway.

H. Thomas Jarrett
C.T. Male Associates
Glens Falls, New York

Dear Mr. Jarrett,

I have your bill for $657.25 that came with the yellowing boilerplate blueprint of details for a holding tank and a letter to our contractor, Jack Davis, with New York State Department of Health specifications for a three bedroom house which are readily available free from New York State.

None of what you sent is specifically applicable to our cottage. The person I spoke to in your office said he felt no on-site inspection of our property was necessary. I am at a loss to understand what it is I am expected to pay $657.25 for but because Mr. Davis assures me the charge is in order I am enclosing a check for that amount.

. . .

Boats, even modern ones, are more expensive and less reliable than cars. We own two wooden boats, a 20' clinker-built Lyman about fifty years old and a 1937 mahogany Gar Wood. The Lyman is a replacement for a bigger Lyman that deteriorated in the boatyard where it was stored during a long period during which it was unused.

(Unnamed Boat Shop)
On Lake George, New York

Dear Sir,

Please explain the charge of $519.62 listed as "summer storage" in the bill I have just received for our Lyman. Was that for last summer when you failed to have the boat ready for us to use?

This year I called in mid June. The woman on the phone said she did not think they could have the boat ready by July 4th. I said I'd pick it up instead the following week which I did.

It was irresponsible of you to turn the boat over to me in the condition we found it. As I was leaving with it, you told me that the choke had to be pulled out slightly to keep the engine running when it was idling. Hardly shipshape condition.

The engine began failing shortly after I passed Dome Island as we were crossing the Lake to our cottage on the East side of the Lake, a distance of four miles. We never reached the East shore before the engine quit altogether even though I tried running with the choke "slightly pulled out" as advised. You had obviously never tested the engine. I was left, stranded offshore in a dangerous situation.

I subsequently had the boat put in proper shape at The Pilot Knob Marina, a competent boatyard. They will attest to the boat's poor condition when they got it on the same day you turned it over to me. That was two days before I got your bill for $519.62.

The carburetor had to be rebuilt, the bilge cleaned of leaves and debris and the water pump replaced. In addition, they put in a new floor carpet and cushions—work that was to have been done by you. The work was completed within a week.

The boat had been stored in your shed for eight years. Storage bills were all paid promptly. When I went to inspect the boat two years ago,

I was appalled that you had let it deteriorate so badly and brought it to your attention. For what I paid, I had a right to expect, clean, dry, indoor storage. The boat was stored under an open shed almost unprotected from the elements. Four inches of water had accumulated in its bottom.

Knowing of your personal problems, I discounted your carelessness and asked if the boat could be restored. I was told it could be readily put back in good shape. It was more than two years after that, during which time I paid your company more than $7,000, that I got the boat back in unseaworthy condition.

Enclosed is my check for $51 for twenty-nine gallons of gas you put in on July 7th.

CC: John Pike (lawyer)

. . .

One of the perquisites of age is getting to call your doctor by his first name.

February 27, 1993

Dr. Paul Beres
Internal Medicine Associates
Westport, Connecticut

Dear Paul,

Thanks for your call after my CAT scan. I'm always pleased by a call from a doctor even if it's with bad news.

Something's going on down there in my stomach whether the CAT scan shows it or not. There are things a person knows about himself that a CAT scan will never tell a doctor. I don't think it's serious. It has something to do with putting food or even drink in my stomach and it only comes when I'm on my feet, standing or walking. I play tennis regularly and, while I've had the ache a few times while playing, it is not induced by it. I cannot put my finger on any one thing that brings on the stomach ache. This morning I stood in a Radio Shack for 20 minutes while someone explained a piece of equipment to me and by the time I got to the car I was retching. First time that's happened although the frequency of the problem doesn't seem to have increased. I'll go for days without it. If I get it and sit down the symptom disappears in minutes.

It is very like what I experienced before Mal fixed my last hernia. I'm convinced I have another rent in my intestinal walls down there somewhere, whether you call it a hernia or not. Would diverticula alone produce stomach pain like that? If it was diverticulitis, would sitting down alleviate it? I'll get your answer at my next visit . . . although I don't think "visit" is the right word for going to see a doctor.

This isn't inhibiting me from doing anything. I don't mean to make a big deal of it. I'm just curious and it is definitely something. I'll keep track and be back to you in a few weeks.

. . .

June 3, 1993

Paul Beres, MD
Internal Medicine Associates
Westport, Connecticut

Dear Paul,

It has been a month now since my hernia operation. Because I know you were puzzled about my problem, you might want to feed my experience into the retrieval system in your brain for future reference: I have had no recurrence of my abdominal discomfort—stomach ache—since the operation.

I could always sense it coming on as long as 20 minutes in advance and I have not had that sensation. It always happened when I was on my feet, walking or standing for an extended period, usually after eating. Last Saturday I worked in my shop for three hours after lunch. Nothing.

I have made my own diagnosis and am pleased to conclude that you were wrong: the pain *was* related to my hernia.

I am also pleased to have you as my doctor.

. . .

Lunsford Richardson, Jr.
Rowayton, Connecticut

Dear Lump,

When anyone asks me to do something on the phone, I always ask them to write me hoping that the effort will be too much for them and they'll drop their request. My ploy failed in your case. I got your letter.

I feel an obligation to our community and I know you've made a major contribution to it over the years and I'd like to help—so, yes. If you'd like me to talk for 20 minutes, I can do that.

My best to Bea.

Residents of our town objected to the location of a strip club, and tried to enlist my help.

Father Michael A. Boccaccio
Saint Phillip Church
Norwalk, Connecticut

Dear Father Boccaccio,

Maybe the best place for The Zebra Club *is* near the church. It might discourage attendance at the club and encourage attendance at the church. Offensive as that kind of enterprise is, I think I'd rather have it near the church than near a lot of other things that might be more influenced by its proximity than the church will be.

Fight it but I don't think it's serious.

. . .

Dear Mr. Kross,

You do a good job as head of the committee that maintains the cemetery and I'm pleased you liked my report.

I don't think I could stand such daily proximity to my future as you have in your job. It's hard not to think of things I'd rather not think about and we're all regularly reminded of death every time we pass the cemetery in town.

I drive by two very old burial grounds on a road I travel in upstate New York. One of them is next to a tumbledown old wreck of a house whose owner has total disregard for the sanctity of the graveyard, piling junk all along its borders and even leaning old car parts against the tombstones nearest his land. He seems immune to the idea that he will soon be a part of it.

I've often wondered how the people buried here would feel about the proximity of the junk the living have left near their last resting place. For all I know, they might like it better than being left alone in a field with nothing but the other dead in sight. Practically, of course, I know they don't feel anything.

Cemeteries are inadequate for their purpose. Somewhere there ought to be a catalog with a brief description of the life and times of everyone who has ever lived. It would mean more than a stone in a field with a name chiseled on it.

No memorial is satisfactory. No building, no marble slab, no plaque, no angel carved in stone preserves the memory of a life as a few paragraphs in a library-of-the-dead would.

. . .

John C. Shaw III
West Yarmouth, Massachusetts

Dear Jack,

We were delighted to hear from you after all these years. Keep in mind I think of you more often than you think of me because I think of you every time I pass the house you lived in as our neighbor for so many years and I pass it at least once a day weekdays and ten times on Saturdays.

The neighborhood is marginally improved over when you were part of it. Some of the houses across the street from you have been nicely fixed up and the dilapidated apartment house down the street is less of a shambles than it used to be. And, of course, there are not so many loud noises emanating in the middle of the night from the White's house since Ed died and he stopped fighting with Norma Jean.

A couple of years ago we bought the LeVay house when Mrs. Levay moved up with her daughter in Andover. You may recall it had a vacant lot next to it and it was one of the last vacant lots left in town. We hated to see them all disappear. We've seen so many ticky tack houses squeezed into the small lots around us, that we were determined it wasn't going to happen there. Margie got an architect to design an extension to the porch that intrudes on the vacant lot and we put a covenant on it which we trust will preclude anyone from building on it in the future. The rebuilt house looks good but I'm glad we didn't plan to retire on the money we make by renting it. On today's market it's worth about three quarters of what we paid and put into it.

A couple of years ago I got a fascinating letter from someone named Funk who had lived up Hunt Street. He knew all about our house. It was built by the Pepper family in the 1860s and it included all the land that the houses that surround us, including yours, are on. Mr. Funk said that during the 1930s, The Depression, the house was an empty derelict. He said his sister got permission from the bank that had taken it over, to house the itinerant men (my father, uncharitably, called them "bums") who had hitched a ride on the train and jumped off at Rowayton. She laid out blankets on the floor for them to sleep on and brought food for them. When you see the Christmases we have in that house, its past is hard to imagine.

The people behind us are good neighbors, Barbara and Ed Wright. They came right after you and Nonie left. He's a very good classical guitarist and Barbara teaches.

We see a lot of Frank and Valle Fay. Frank is the star reporter for *The Hour* and a Norwalk treasure because he knows everything about everyone. I can hardly wait to die to see his obit on me.

Kiggins must be doing well. I count eleven oil trucks down there by his fuel company office these days. They hate a nice warm winter like the one we had this year.

Ray Street finally converted the garage and rented it to a Fred Astaire franchise operation although I've never seen anyone in there dancing.

The Cohn's have been great, stable neighbors. The people in the big Victorian house opposite us—he was some kind of graphic artist—had a terrible time and finally lost the place to the bank about six months ago.

Some woman up that street opposite our driveway—where the barns used to be and the tacky houses now abound—committed suicide last year. It's strange we can live in such proximity to someone and be unaware that they are desparate.

There are, however, a lot fewer fires in town since they caught that kid who was setting them many years ago. It's a trade-off because it makes life in town less exciting.

Rowayton has been surprisingly stable. We have many of the same friends we had within a year or two of moving there in 1951. I like that kind of stability even though we often go months without seeing a lot of them.

The kids are all good and successful. We don't send money. We're all in touch with each other, all the way around, several times a week. Ellen went to London to work for ABC four years ago, met an Englishman and married him. We all like him a lot. El is working as a photographer. She has the cover on the Fodor guide to Prague. How's that for fame?

Emily lives in Boston. She's news director of WCVB. Martha's in Washington and Brian is an ABC correspondent in Los Angeles. They come for Christmas and for two weeks in the summer and we go to London once a year—or Margie does anyway. Ellen sort of abandoned an apartment in New York and we ended up taking it over and giving her some money to buy a place there. It's on the Upper West Side, not a garden spot, but we like it and use it once a week or so. It's cheap and convenient.

Emily's coming down from Boston this afternoon. I'm a presenter for the duPont Columbia Awards tonight and, unbeknownst to her, she's getting one and I've been asked to present it to her. It'll be fun.

Tomorrow we're going to Los Angeles for the Super Bowl. Brian, who was finally married last summer at our place in the country, lives in Hollywood. We'll go to the game together. I wrote an article for the Super Bowl program this year. They offered me $3500 for it but I said I had $3500. What I didn't have was a ticket to the game, a plane ride out there or a hotel room. They gave me all that for the article. It's about the most I've ever been paid.

Martha lives in Chevy Chase and has a good job with the National Institute of Health. She has two sons, Em has a daughter.

The last time we were on Cape Cod we had dinner with Kurt Vonnegut. It was a long time ago. I remember it well because, when I asked Kurt how he was doing as a freelance writer, he said "Good. I made the same as the high school principle here last year, $5,600."

You didn't know what you were in for when you wrote.

Pass along our best wishes to Nonie.

Angela Nicolaysen
Weichert Realtors
Mendham, New Jersey

Dear Angela,

Thank you for your letter, sent to my home in Connecticut, offering me two homes in Mendham, N.J. for either $2,450,000 or $2,550,000. If I take both of them, do I get anything off? From the pictures you

sent along with your letter, I can't tell the difference between the two houses. Why is one so cheap?

You refer to the houses as "homes" or "residences." "A house" as someone famous once said "is not a home." When the builder finishes it and it's sitting there empty, as the places in the pictures were, it's neither a residence nor a home. It's a house. I know "home" is a more attractive word for you real estate salesmen but it isn't a home until someone moves in and puts their own junk in the garage.

I bring this up because you real estate people don't always state things accurately. I will concede that you women in real estate are special. You're often attractive and well-dressed but you could stand being more bashful than you are.

I've been trying to figure out why you chose me to send your sales letter to. The only thing I can think is, you drove by our house and decided we could afford better.

That's a pretty insulting thing for you to do, Angela. Yes, the placc needs a little work but I'll be getting at that, probably, as soon as my vacation is over. I know, for instance, that the side of the garage door looks bad where someone knocked off the molding. There are other places where some paint wouldn't hurt. The gutters on the side need replacing, I know that.

Your letter reminded me that it wouldn't do any harm if I had a couple of loads of topsoil brought in so I could reseed the lawn and get more real grass growing there.

The day you drove past there may have been a beer can down front. Kids do that driving by once in a while but listen, Angela, what's a banged up garage door, a bad paint job, some rusty gutters, a lawn with some bare spots and a beer can or two compared with $2,550,000?

There are several other things in your letter I want to mention to you. You say Mendham and the surrounding communities "have long

been associated with people of achievement and prestige." You point out that the area has "enticed a number of celebrities, among them Whitney Houston, Jacqueline Onassis, Mike Tyson and Malcolm Forbes."

I want to be honest with you Angela, I've made good money the last ten years but I don't have the kind of money Jackie, Whitney and Malcolm have and having Mike Tyson as a neighbor is not all that compelling a feature of the neighborhood to me.

Your letter is a persuasive sales pitch, but I do have some advice for you in that regard. You say that "This sophisticated, yet quaint rural environment is enhanced by its proximity to New York City only 50 minutes away and easily accessible by car, train or bus."

The minute you bring up the specter of a bus ride into New York, you destroy the image you have tried so hard to create. If I moved out there, would I see Jacqueline Onassis, Mike Tyson or Malcolm Forbes on the bus coming into New York? I think your letter should read "easily accessible by limousine."

We paid $29,500 for our home and we've been in it since 1951. I'm not a potential customer.

PART THIRTEEN

Friends (and Enemies)

Oram Clark Hutton was a major figure in my life while I was learning the newspaper business. I could not have had a better, tougher teacher. We ended up friends and co-authors of three books, one of which sold to MGM. He was known far and wide as "Bud."

We corresponded, partially in a kind of shorthand, until he died in 1984.

September 1959

O.C. Hutton
Easton, Maryland

Dear Bud,

When we first met, you were twenty-nine and talked a lot about what you had done with your life. I being only five, or is it six, years younger and having done nothing of great interest with my life, resented your suggestion that any appreciable portion of yours was over. I certainly didn't think mine was because it hadn't started.

You don't get to worry any more about age I don't think. Stop it for [illegible] I remember worrying about dying when I was eight. I knew everyone had always died up 'til then but I entertained the hope that my Mother, my dog Spike and I would be the first exceptions. That all changed when Spike died and I realized I probably wasn't going to live forever either.

Once a month I get a seeping feeling—"seeping" is it?—in my gut from thinking of death and nothing ever again. Nothing, ever. Death must get easier when you're closer to it. I hope so. The tougher death is the easier it would be to let go, I suppose.

Last weekend I went out to SAC Headquarters in Omaha. Big airplanes. Bigger by a lot than the B17s we knew. They're the answer I guess. Le May was there. He's good I guess. Not good but good for the job. I wish he didn't have that knack for getting as much publicity as he does and at the same time, making little asides about how much he hates publicity.

Le May came up on a stage in front of 3000 people, went over to Jimmy Stewart who had introduced him and whispered to Stewart that he would not say anything. I was close enough to hear him. If he didn't want to speak or be seen, not being there at all would have served the same end if that was really his end. Not saying anything I mean.

I see Benny, Charley. Mazo has gone to Washington. Bob's suit is spottier, teeth rottener and when he talks to you he spends more time than ever looking over your shoulder for someone who has never yet come in the door when I was with him. What is it he looks at over your shoulder? He comes to work at about 11:45 and stops by Bleecks for a couple of martinis before going upstairs to the city room at the *Trib*.

After he checks in to see what's happening, he comes back down to Bleecks for lunch but he doesn't eat anything, he just has two more martinis.

He goes back in until about four when he takes a break and comes back down. I cannot understand how he's as good a newspaperman as he is.

Bob hangs out a lot with John Lardner, Dick Maney, John Crosby and Red Smith. I see them all but don't feel like one of the crowd.

I am immensely happy except when I'm thinking about death and I may be fooling myself but if so I am doing such a good job it doesn't matter.

Alfred Balk
Syracuse University

Dear Al,

Thanks for remembering I was interested in getting a copy of your book. What I've read of it is good news to me—if it's true.

I'm constantly on the lookout for news that offers hope to mankind, the United States or to me personally. For instance, I save stories that say that chocolate ice cream counters any tendency a man has toward baldness—something like that.

In a more important way, your book with such good evidence that America isn't falling apart, fits into that category. I'm factoring it in to my general sense of well-being and satisfaction with what's happening here.

I am not so sanguine as you are, though. I'm obsessed with the notion that we've become a nation of salesmen. We're selling it better than we're making it.

We had dinner with Isaac and Janet Asimov at our home in Rensselaerville a few weeks ago. His brain hasn't deteriorated but his body isn't what it was—and it was never much. Janet is a charming hypochondriac with a medical education which is the worst kind.

Mrs. Paul McArdle
Chevy Chase, Maryland

Dear Angela,

Charley and your son both called with the bad news. I hope it was Pops who saw it coming and asked that I be told of his death.

Paul was "Pops" to all of us on the football team where we got to be such close friends. I don't know who starts nicknames but it's interesting how often a person becomes inseparable from one. I never think of Paul as anything but "Pops" and I've thought of him a lot over the years. I've been proud to know him every time I read a story in the *Washington Post* about some judicial decision he handed down. I've thought of him often when I'm writing, too. Sometimes I use too many contractions in my work and they remind me that "Pops" never used any, either in writing or in speech. It gave the statements he made great impact even when they were of no great consequence. "I am pleased to see you," he would say. Never "I'm."

I wish now that we had seen more of each other through the years. It's too bad good friends drift apart. We move, we acquire different interests and make new friends. We don't forget old friends once we make new ones but we make more than we can keep.

No one who ever knew "Pops" at The Academy will ever forget his effervescent sense of humor and his class as a gentleman.

. . .

Robert Schuller
Crystal Cathedral
California

Dear Bob,

You ought to know that you're the best friend of all the friends I have, who is a minister. This is a position once occupied by Eugene Carson Blake who was the head Presbyterian in this Country. (His title was "Stated Clerk" which surely doesn't sound as good as "Pope" or even "Monsignor.") Gene was a good guy and, because he'd played at Princeton, took on the job as part-time line coach of the football team where I went to school in Albany. I always told people he taught me how to play football dirty.

You say that any time I'm in the area "WE'D—like to have you visit us."

I'm never sure about that political "we" you use but I would like to talk with you sometime. Only you though. I don't want to talk to "we." You sound like a good guy. "WE," I'm not so sure about.

I'm pleased to hear that you and God, to whom you say you're so close, both love me although I'm worried about what the two of you would think if you knew me better.

If you decide to leave the church, call me. I'll try to talk you out of it.

. . .

Max Weitz
Fort Lee, New Jersey

Dear Max,

It was fun getting that bit of memorabilia noting my acceptance into membership at the Business Men's Club of the West Side YMCA in 1951.

We had some great times there and some great handball. Our group usually consisted of Tony Marvin, Godfrey's announcer, Tom Lockard of "The Mariners" quartet, Chuck Horner, a writer, and me.

Fred Allen hung out there a lot. One day he told the story about Frankie, the former featherweight boxer and later hyperactive runner for JP Morgan. He used to get rich customers through customs in a hurry. Frankie was always on the go himself. Couldn't stand still. He was playing handball in a foursome with Fred when one of the men, an overweight dentist named Eisenman, slumped to the floor with a heart attack. Fred said Frankie bolted out the door into the hall and the other two figured everything would be okay because Frankie was going to get a doctor.

Thirty seconds later, they heard Frankie in the locker room yelling "Hey, we need a fourth in here? Anybody want to fill in?"

. . .

Duke Drake
Wickenburg, Arizona

Dear Duke,

If I'd never heard of you at Colgate, no one who ever spent more than ten minutes with Wally Powell would have gone without knowing a lot about you. He talked about you all the time and listening to him I regretted not having known you better in college.

Wally must have been seventy-two or seventy-three when I first met him. He's the oldest good friend I ever made and I never had a better one.

We spent a lot of time together every week for ten glorious summers and had more fun together with a variety of woodworking projects than I can describe to you.

We'd often take off across the countryside in my old Ford Station Wagon, looking for some small sawmill we'd heard of and we invariably came home with the car loaded with cherry, maple and walnut. Some days I'd have to unload all of it at our house and wait until Roma went out of their house before I could deliver Wally's wood to him. Roma didn't take kindly to his hobby and barely tolerated me for encouraging him in it.

Wally had no patience with finishing or sanding but he made some nice pieces of furniture and nothing was too difficult for him to attempt. He could follow directions or a pattern. I could not. His Queen Anne armchair was way beyond my ability. The compound angles on the arms alone were confounding and he hand-carved the ball-and-claw feet himself.

I'll always miss him.

. . .

Durward Kirby
Sanibel, Florida

Dear Durward,

It's been hard to write you because I know you haven't been having a good time and Garry Moore's death is too sad for either of us to think about, let alone write about. If there was a world's champion of Good Guys, Garry would have been it.

Garry's son called me the morning he died and I was pleased to be included on the list he made of friends to be called. I stopped being angry with cigarette smokers a long while ago and started feeling sorry for them instead. Cronkite saw Garry within the last few months and said he'd turn off his oxygen tank for long enough to have a smoke and then turn it back on.

I often recall what fun we had doing those radio shows. You were so good at taking a script cold and making more out of it than I had written into it. You and Garry could hardly have been a better combination.

Five years writing a ten-minute-a-day program produced a large volume of scripts which I've had nicely bound—not that I think posterity gives a damn.

It would be good to see you but unlikely. I'm one of those people who revels in not liking Florida.

. . .

Fred Friendly
New York Hospital

Dear Fred,

There was a kind of silence from your direction so I called Natalie and got the news. She was good at giving it but I couldn't tell whether the news was good or bad. She reported that you have "spinal spinosis" which sounds redundant. The closest my dictionary comes to spinosis is "Spinosity: something that is nettlesome or difficult."

You certainly have that. No one is more nettlesome and difficult than you are.

Just below that is "spinoxism: the philosophy of Spinoza who taught that reality is one substance with an infinite number of attributes of which only thought is capable of being apprehended by the human mind."

You clearly have that, too.

Call if you need flowers, cookies or conversation.

We'll be thinking of you until you get over whatever it is you have and won't stop thinking of you then, either . . .

Barry Goldwater
Scottsdale, Arizona

Dear Barry,

A letter from you gives my mail more class than it normally has. I got it shortly after admiring your performance with Larry King. I don't think of myself as a big Larry King fan but he does a good job. He asks good questions, he listens to answers and he isn't trying to make any points of his own.

I agree with you that it doesn't make sense to include women and to exclude gays in the military.

It's interesting to consider what your life would be like now if you'd been elected President in 1964. Not as good, probably. I guess you can thank me for not having voted for you.

. . .

Margaret Suh
Op-Ed Page
San Francisco Chronicle

Dear Margaret,

Yes, I can say a few words about Herb Caen.

I had not seen a lot of Herb over the years but we'd been together two or three times a year for the past thirty years and the times we had together were extraordinarily good. It was one of the things about Herb—times with him were good. You didn't have to see him every day to know him well.

Herb and I returned to the beaches of Normandy with a group of newspaper reporters on three of the even-numbered anniversaries of

D-Day. We took a side trip to Brussels on one of those occasions and six of us went to dinner at one of Belgium's good restaurants. We were sitting facing each other, three on a side, in a banquette with the oblong table between us. It was good for conversation and the conversation was good until William Randolph Hearst, Jr. came in the door.

Bill Hearst was friendly and he knew everyone at the table—Hal Boyle, Bob Considine among them—and he walked up and shook hands with five of us. He acted as if Herb wasn't there.

After some inconsequential chatter, Hearst left.

"What was that all about?" Hal asked Herb. "He never spoke to you."

"No" Herb laughed. "He hasn't spoken to me since the day I left the *Examiner* for the *Chronicle* and his circulation dropped 40,000 the next morning."

A lot of the memorable times I had with Herb were while we were eating.

At "21" in New York, years ago when the popularity of the Caesar salad was still largely a California phenomenon, Herb was in from San Francisco for a few days and ordered one. When the salad came the greens looked good but it was not a Caesar salad in the California tradition. Herb demanded to talk to the chef. He was having fun with it but he wanted to talk to the chef. The chef came out in his touque blanche and black and white checked trousers and stood by our table as they argued about the ingredients in a Caesar salad.

"Get me a telephone" Herb said. The head waiter plugged in a phone, Herb dialed a long number and finally got the chef in one of his favorite San Francisco restaurants. He spoke with him briefly and then handed the phone to the chef at "21."

"Here" Herb said, "he'll tell you how to make a Caesar salad."

One of the last times I saw Herb was in San Francisco when he took me to lunch with his friend, Willie Brown. It was a year before Willie became mayor. Herb and Willie were very good friends and they were good for each other. Willie was an invaluable source of information for Herb, as I'm sure you know and Herb didn't do Willie's political career any harm.

I haven't talked to Willie since Herb died but I'll bet tears came to Willie's eyes, too. It wasn't all business between them.

. . .

This was written to friends, an art literate couple, late at night following a three-hour visit to the Museum of Modern Art to see the Matisse exhibit and a long dinner with them afterwards during which we argued about art and exhibitions.

1:45 A.M.

Dear Sarah and Jim,

I haven't been able to sleep partly because of too much wine and partly because I was uneasy about our argument. While they're still in my mind, I'm going to try to put down what I thought about the Matisse exhibit less incoherently than I did in conversation.

My complaint was not with Matisse but with the museum's presentation of his art.

I recognize the importance to civilization of an appreciation of good art but as you surely noticed tonight, art appreciation is not something that comes naturally to me. Given the opportunity to attend a performance at the Metropolitan Opera, an exhibition of Abstract Expressionism or a New York Giants football game, I would choose to go to the game. I realize this is a know-nothing attitude but I can't help myself.

Driven by my sense I'm wrong, I often attend some cultural event or go to a museum as we did tonight. I was willing to go because for the past several months it has been impossible to go to a party in New York without being asked "Have you been to the Matisse exhibit?"

Well thanks to you and Margie, next time I'm asked, I can say I have been. From the bitter experience of not being able to remember what I've just seen when I sit down to write, I often offend people at social gatherings by scribbling notes on scraps of paper. You probably noticed me doing it tonight. I've been looking them over.

My first note is "HEADSETS."

When we first came into the Museum, they were offering guided tours on tape. You could rent a headset and a tape player if you wished to be guided. The idea of listening to what someone else has to say or thinks about what I am looking at is offensive to me and I was pleased that neither you or Jim rented one.

"WHO NAMED?" I've written because I wondered who decided to call Matisse's paintings by the names on them. Did Matisse name them or does the museum do that? The names are good. Very simple and direct. "Woman in a Flowered Hat," "Open Door—Brittany," etc.

The writing on the wall next to the pictures was poor as literature or information. I've noted phrases like "conflating these elements. . . ," "architectonic style." Is there a dictionary around the museum for the Giants fans?

One read "Matisse's naturalism disguises an underlying abstraction . . ." If you'll pardon the dated expression, Baloney!

Another was described as having "an almost neo-classical quality." Why don't they let us just look at the pictures and decide for ourselves what they have?

I'm always doubtful when a critic calls a work "neo" anything. Especially if it's only "almost" neo.

How long did it take Henri to run these up? Why don't they tell us that on the wall if they want to tell us something? I wish they'd gotten Johnny Apple to write the copy. He'd have told us what we wanted to know. Did it take Matisse an hour to paint these? A day? A month? How long? Give us some information!

I tried to pick up some phrases by listening to some of those people around us who know them. You heard that one woman say of Matisse "He was well-sold in his lifetime." I think that's one. . . a phrase, I could use at my next museum visit I mean. I liked hearing of an artist who didn't starve in a garret, though.

Are any of these paintings bad? Fair maybe? They aren't all great, are they? They look great but I can't tell the good ones from the great ones or the junk. Was there ever an artist who didn't do some bad work? Which ones of these aren't too good? Why aren't they? It's frustrating that I don't know. This is my lack of education in art showing and there must be others like me so why don't they give us some help?

I couldn't help noticing that Matisse didn't paint many men. It's my impression that most artists haven't. You'd probably know and I should have asked you last night. Has there ever been a great woman artist who dwelt on the bodies of men?

Male nudes are nuder than women nudes, of course, maybe that accounts for it. Men have more to hide.

One of my notes just says "PINEAPPLES." Pineapples are more popular with artists than with eaters, I think. There's often one in a picture. Cezanne, Picasso. . . they all did pineapples.

It's funny when you consider it because most people now buy pineapple with a hole in the middle cut out by machine at the canning factory. I guess a can of pineapple doesn't do much for an artist.

"CLOSER" I noted. I meant that it seemed as though I was standing closer to these paintings than most people so I stepped back. I didn't want to look as though I was from out of town.

I must have been standing about where Matisse stood when he painted them, though. How wrong could that have been?

I loved some of the pictures. Too much though. I was tired of standing, tired of looking. The program said there are 412 of Matisse's works here. If I had spent thirty seconds looking at each one—which isn't enough—and an average of five seconds to get from one to the next, that comes to a little more than four hours.

I never think of myself as being alive while any of the great artists were still painting but Matisse didn't die until I was thirty-five. I didn't know what to make of that.

Matisse's handwriting was very good and legible but his lines all go uphill like mine. You'd think anyone as good as he was at putting a line precisely where he wanted it with paint on a canvas could control his handwriting better to keep it from going uphill.

There's no question it was too much of one thing though. Like listening to all nine Beethoven Symphonies at one sitting.

There was a painting called "Chinese Fish." Why did Matisse think he knew the fish were Chinese? It reminds me of the story of the two Chinese philosophers standing on the bridge looking into the water.

"See how the fish dart about" said the first philosopher "that is the happiness of the fish."

"You not being a fish " said the other "how can you know the fish are happy?"

"Aha!" said the first philosopher. "You, not being I, cannot know that I don't know that the fish are happy."

Matisse not being a fish, how did he know they were Chinese?

I don't get the impression Henri was a lot of fun to be around. He looks kind of stuffy in the paintings he did of himself. You don't catch him in his shirtsleeves. Why would a guy paint a self-portrait of himself in his best suit?

But this is all quibbling because I couldn't sleep. It was a memorable evening but I want you to remember that my going to it is more of a concession to art than art lovers are willing to make to football games. I've been to museums all over the world but I never see any art lovers out at Giants stadium.

PART FOURTEEN

Written But Not Mailed

Even though I've written a lot of letters, there are many letters I've always wanted to write but did not. I set out to do it just for fun one day.

These are all letters I never wrote.

Dear Editor,

In the past year, I have written five letters to you but the paper has not printed a single one. They were all more interesting than the letters you have used. I think you are prejudiced against me because I am a minority—a normal, average, every-day American.

Dear Mr. Mayor,

I read in the paper where you said you were going to eliminate a lot of desk jobs in the police force and put more cops out on the street. I have checked my records and you said the same thing in 1979, 1983, 1987, 1992 and last October.

Dear President Clinton,

You're making it very difficult for me to be happy I voted for you.

James Weirton
President
First National Bank

Dear Sir,

Please ask the people who mail me my bank statement to stop putting a lot of junk in with it. My statement saying how much money I have is all I want.

If you insist on sending junk mail, please send it in a separate envelope, clearly marked "JUNK MAIL," so I can throw it out without opening it.

Your free offer of a wonderful new credit card came this morning and I want to ask about that, too.

Why is it any better than my old credit card?

It has been my experience that if a bank makes me an offer, there's more in it for the bank than there is for me.

Edward L. Cameron
College Alumni Association

Dear Ed,

A good way to raise money for the college would be for the Fund Raising office to stop wasting it on stamps asking me for more after I've already given. I only give once a year, if that, and no number of requests, expensive brochures or schedules of football games will cause me to increase the amount.

Over the years, you have sent me hundreds of letters asking for money and explaining the wonderful plans the college has for a new dormitory, a new biology building, a new gym.

Why is it necessary for the college to get any bigger? It was okay the way it was. Instead of putting up a lot of new buildings, you might consider tearing some of the old ones down. With the money you save in upkeep, maybe you could send us loyal alumni a refund.

Dear Editor,

Why didn't you run my angry letter about all the angry letters I've written that you haven't run in your newspaper?

Angrily,

Dear Mr. Morrison,

I have received the manuscript of your novel which you asked me to read and evaluate.

You say you have sent your book to five publishers, all of whom sent it back. This *is* an evaluation, Mr. Morrison and it sounds to me as though your novel isn't any good.

Doesn't it occur to you that it's an imposition to ask a stranger to spend twenty hours reading a book of yours that no one will publish?

Dear Magazine Subscription Manager,

No, I do not want to buy a ten-year subscription to your magazine at a savings of $142.85.

Under separate cover, please just send me $142.85.

PART FIFTEEN

Faith in Reason

Frank A. Karwoski
Red Bud, Illinois

Dear Mr. Karwoski,

Thank you for your interest in saving my soul.

I would think it is probable that I have given a great deal more thought to the possibility there is a God than you have given to the likelihood that there is not one. I hope you don't think this all-powerful God, who must have provided me with my doubts if he is all-powerful, would then proceed to punish me for the doubts I have.

Robert Bittick
Carmel, California

Dear Mr. Bittick,

No responsible authority on the bible contends that Matthew, Mark, Luke and John were all apostles. Two may have been. One probably was.

There are serious questions about which, if any, of the "gospel writers," actually had anything to do with writing the gospel. It's a quagmire. There are bible students who contend that what purports to be from "Matthew" was actually written by committee and "Matthew" was a name they gave it, not a byline. Matthew apparently had put down notes and some of them were used but he was probably dead by the time the gospel named "Matthew" was assembled.

There's such confusion in the gospels themselves that they don't help us sort it out. On the cross, did Jesus say "My God, my God why have you forsaken me?" As it says in Mark and Matthew? Or did he say, as according to Luke "Father forgive them etc.?" Or did John get it right when he quotes Jesus as saying "It is finished."

But, I mean, I don't know. All I know is there are a thousand theories and I tend not to believe any of them. If you're comfortable with one and it makes you happy, believe.

Don Jonas
North Hollywood, California

Dear Mr. Jonas,

Judaism, as you say, is a religion but there doesn't seem to be any universally held opinion about exactly what Jews are. No dictionary I have, limits its definition of a Jew to someone who believes in Judaism.

I have many friends who, by all other standards are Jewish, but who are agnostics. How do you handle that? Was Sammy Davis, Jr. really Jewish because he said he was and embraced Judaism? I don't think so.

After Mike Wallace did a report on *60 Minutes* that angered many Jews, I met a friend who worked for the Jewish Defense League. He was angry because Mike hadn't replied to a critical letter he'd written.

I said "Listen—every time Mike Wallace does a piece, he gets 5,000 letters and, if it's about Jews, he gets 10,000."

My friend snapped back, "That's because Jews are twice as literate."

I agree.

T.O. Shanavas
Adrian, Michigan

Dear Dr. Shanavas,

If your letter had not so exasperated me I would have smiled and thrown it in the wastebasket.

How do I respond to someone who says black is white and elephants are camels? What do I say to defend myself against someone who quotes me as saying outrageous things I did not say?

I did not say, "The Koran teaches to kill non-Muslims."

I did not say, "Koran says only Muslims go to heaven."

Should I, perhaps, say to you "Dear Dr. Shanavas, I am shocked by the allegations in your letter in which you say that Christians want to kill all Muslims. Why do you claim that the Bible says that only Jews go to heaven? I am shocked that you contend that "the Bible teaches violence against Islam."

Such a letter would be comparable to your letter to me. It is difficult to understand how someone whose status in society suggests he has some intelligence, could write such a hopelessly illogical letter. I can only think that your mastery of English is not so good as your relatively neat typing of it would suggest.

I did say that very little is known about most of Mohammed's life. If you know of his life, I'd be interested in hearing in some detail what he was doing and who his acquaintances were when he was thirty-one and thirty-two years old.

Your comment about the Bible suggests that you think I would defend it in comparison with the Koran. While I concede it is difficult to retain any poetic beauty in anything that's been translated from another language, the Bible has retained a lot; the Koran very little that I can discern from the English translation I have.

You suggest that I misunderstand the Koran when I suggest it is a violent, repugnant book in many ways. May I quote: (Sura iii 56):

"As to those who reject faith
I will punish them
With terrible agony
In this world and in the Hereafter
Nor will they have
Anyone to help."

(The word hereafter was actually capitalized, to give you some idea of the intellectual level of this translation.)

Or, Sura iv 18 (speaking of those who reject belief):

". . . for them
Have we prepared
A punishment most grievous."

Sura iv 151:

"And we have prepared
For Unbelievers a humiliating
Punishment."

There are hundreds, perhaps thousands, of such uncivilized warnings in the Koran and I cannot imagine reading it as anything but interesting mythology.

You quote a book written by a history professor in 1876. Has anything been written on the subject since the invention of the vacuum cleaner?

Your letter suggests so much difference in how we think—or, indeed, whether we think—that I despair, if we are typical, of our two worlds ever understanding each other.

In 1989 I put down some of my thoughts on religion for our children.

Dear Ellen, Martha, Emily and Brian,

During the several thousand dinner table conversations we had when you were growing up, we talked about almost everything and inevitably religion was one of the subjects that came up. Because the conversations were usually short and inconclusive, I never laid out what I believe or don't believe in any orderly way, and I wanted to put down some of my thoughts on the subject now that you are grown.

I had originally thought of it as a letter to you about religion but I realized, after I wrote most of it, that it is not a letter. It doesn't have the style or the casual familiarity of a letter. It's a rambling set of notes and if they are not always clear, it is because I am not always clear what I think about religion. I'm not the only one.

Do what you want with them. I hope you'll read them but then, save them or throw them out. I'm not sure anyone would ever want to publish them.

One frustrating thing about religion to me, as a reporter, is that unlike any other subject, if you approach it with an open mind, you are considered to be biased against it.

If you apply the same reason and logic to religion that you use in assessing everything else in your life, you're considered an agnostic at best and an atheist at worst.

Generally speaking, religious people have been more vocal about what they believe than skeptics have about what they doubt. When I'm in someone's home and they say a prayer before we eat, I don't stand up and say "Wait a minute. Why are you forcing this on me ? I think it's nonsense!"

I go to dinners in hotel banquet rooms where a minister or priest asks people to bow their heads while he speaks. There must be others in the room who think it's as offensive as I do but no one ever walks out or stands up and states the case for disbelief.

There are a great many closet atheists or agnostics in the academic world who don't say anything, either. Professors give students their best advice on everything except religion. They shy away from it for fear of offending students, parents or the college administration.

I've never said much about religion in public myself. I don't write or talk about it because most of the people who like what I do on television and write in my column, would not like what I think about religion. I don't know whether I'm being dishonest or polite. If I can do any good with what I write—every writer dreams of having something good come out of what he or she does—losing an audience would end that. I hide behind the popular idea that "Religion is a person's own business." Most people don't really believe that. They just say it.

How this Earth and all the life on it came about is, so far, beyond anyone's ability to understand but it seems wrong to stop trying by saying simply that "it's the work of God." Even if you think God created it, you haven't finished answering the question because you have to follow it up by asking "Then who created God?" It's like astronomers trying to figure out the extent of the universe. They talk about the outside limits of it—the end of it—but if there's an end to it, what's just beyond the end? It's frightening to consider.

That's the reason religion took hold—fear of the unknown. We're afraid in the dark. Make up a story, believe in it and the light comes on and fear disappears. That's religion. It gives believers something to hang onto, an answer to the unanswerable.

I don't differentiate much, except in degree, between people who believe in religion from those who believe in astrology, magic or the supernatural.

I call myself an agnostic, not an atheist because, in one sense atheists are like Christians or Muslims. They're sure of themselves. A Christian says with certainty, there is a God; an atheist says with certainty, there is no God. Neither knows.

I've read about people who left the church who felt a great emptiness in their lives. They rejected religion intellectually but were lost and unhappy without it. Something was missing in their lives. I feel none of that.

George Bernard Shaw said "The fact that a believer is happier than a non-believer is no more to the point than that a drunk is happier than someone who's sober."

I am worried about death but it has nothing to do with my agnosticism. I'd have the same feeling of dread if I was Catholic and went to mass twice a day. If good Catholics really believed in a life hereafter, why would they worry at all about death?

One of the complaints skeptics have about religion is that it has had a negative effect on the progress of civilization. It has provided a false explanation for problems and retarded the search for real answers to others. It slowed science's search for answers to medical problems. It still impedes progress in many areas.

If that wasn't reason enough to doubt religion's benefits to mankind, religion has caused more wars and massacres than dictators, crazy kings or border disputes have.

A lot of people are consoled by the thought that there's some benevolent power who they see in the form of a sort of superperson, looking down on them and controlling their destiny. We all ought to understand we're on our own. Believing in Santa Claus doesn't do kids any harm for a few years but it isn't smart for them to continue waiting all their lives for him to come down the chimney with something wonderful. Santa Claus and God are cousins.

All the ritual and amulets that go with religion help make it attractive. People like getting their hands on little crosses they can hang around their necks to proclaim their affiliation with God to any passer-by who sees them. They can count beads, make the sign of the cross passing a Catholic church or kneel and face Mecca to pray in a mosque. We like what we're familiar with.

It would be wrong and I'd feel bad if I gave the impression that I'm negative about the church in America as a social institution. Churches bind many communities together like nothing else. Once a week people put on their good clothes and go to one place together to do the same thing. They sit side-by-side with friends or strangers with a common purpose. There is nothing else comparable to it as a cohesive force. Neither Rotary, bridge groups, Kiwanis, American Legion, VFW or any private club has the same effect of pulling the community together and giving it a sense of goodness.

The hymns that can be sung in unison by everyone regardless of their musical ability are uplifting even when the words to them are stupefying. I was caught up in the spirit that comes with hymn-singing in chapel at The Albany Academy. I sang two hymns a day, five days a week for eight years growing up and I can still amaze my friends singing the mindless words of at least the first chorus of twenty of them.

"We're gathered together to ask the Lord's blessing."

"Rock of ages, cleft for thee."

Cleft for thee? Don't try to make sense of it, just join in with the feeling of warmth that togetherness brings and sing. I liked it. I still like it.

I just wish this social institution wasn't based on what appears to me to be a monumental hoax built on an accumulation of customs and myths directed toward proving something that isn't true.

People who go to church regularly and believe in God assume they have higher moral standards than those who don't. There are no statistics to support this and there's no evidence that it's true. Christians talk as though goodness was their idea but good behavior doesn't have any religious origin. Our prisons are filled with the devout.

I'd be more willing to accept religion, even if I didn't believe it, if I thought it made people nicer to each other but I don't think it does. I have friends who work on Wall Street and make hard business decisions every day by applying logic and reason to information but they go to church on Sunday and take it all in without a question. Those same businessmen I know who go to church on Sunday, set out Monday morning to cut the throat of their competition.

Fooling people into being virtuous with the promise of heaven or scaring them into it with the threat of hell, doesn't seem like the best way to promote goodness anyway. Not only that, it doesn't work.

It's impossible for anyone to be virtuous all the time because virtue is behaving better than you feel like behaving. Virtue leads to more happiness than unhappiness. That's how virtue got a good name. Christians came along and acted as if they had invented virtue with the rules called "The Ten Commandments." They were allegedly given to Moses, alone with God and under mysterious circumstances, on a mountain that can no longer be located called "Sinai." And I am the Queen of Romania.

There have been a dozen prophets, in the course of history, whose claims that God has revealed his word to them have been taken seriously by large numbers of people. Those to whom his word was revealed were always alone in some remote place, like Moses.

There wasn't anyone else around when Mohammed got the word, either. Mormon, Joseph Smith, and Christian Scientist, Mary Baker Eddy, had exclusive audiences with God. We have to trust them as reporters—and you know how reporters are. They'll do anything for a story.

All these people heard voices, all uncorroborated, that no one else heard and it's hard to imagine God would favor just those few people and a few thousand nuts over the years who have made similar claims. People who pretend to be closer to God than the rest of us are especially irritating because usually they are frauds and quite often they're doing it for money.

The best rules for a successful life have been promoted by all religions but those things were true before there was religion and they'd be true if there were none.

There's nothing mystical about the high regard humans have for being honest, unselfish, caring, brave, generous, faithful, loving.

Thousands of years of experience made it clear, long before the Ten Commandments were set down, that people are more apt to be happy if they are all these things than if they are not.

If people need to have something to make them believe in what's good for them, beyond common sense or what their brains lead them to believe, I suppose it's possible to defend being religious but it's a trick they're playing on themselves and they ought to know it.

I'm puzzled and disappointed to find people I think of as smarter than I am who believe, or act as though they believe, that Mary had a baby without previously having had sex with Joseph or anyone but a ghost.

We have had countless Presidents of the United States, men in whose judgment we trust the future of our Country, who accept the notion that Mary was a virgin somehow made pregnant by "the Holy Ghost." (I'm on dangerous ground here. The Bible says "Whosoever speaketh against the Holy Ghost it shall not be forgiven him neither in this world nor in the world to come." Seems sort of vengeful.)

Bill Buckley is kind of a friend. I like and admire him, wrong as he so frequently is. He's smart and has a command of the English language I envy. He unequivocally accepts as fact, the myth of the virgin birth.

Mary's pregnancy is also called, somewhat pompously, "The Immaculate Conception" as if sex was something dirtier than immaculate. The literature of religion has several stories of virgin births and it seems likely that Christianity borrowed one of those. Considering how vehemently the followers of one religion reject the beliefs of another, it's surprising how much borrowing has gone on, one from another.

Most educated people who are religious don't try to defend their religion or put it to the same objective methods of inquiry that they would apply to anything else in their lives.

That's the only way to be religious that makes sense. Confess to being puzzled about the meaning of life—if there is any—and say, in effect "It beats the hell out of me. I don't know but I want something to hang onto so I take God. Don't ask me to make sense of it."

The other thing people say who can't accept the illogic of religion is "I'm not religious in the traditional sense." They say that because they don't dare announce that they don't believe even though they have a feeling that it's unbelievable.

There are thoughtful people who laugh at the newspaper report of a weeping stone virgin in the backyard of a house in Newark, but accept tenets of their religion which are as hard for a rational person to believe as a stone that cries.

One of the good things to be said is that there is a certain element of modesty in the most religious among us. People are unsure of themselves. They worry that if their lives depend on the decisions they make with the brains they have, they aren't up to it. They're afraid they aren't smart enough to handle everything.

If, on the other hand, their lives depend not on themselves but on hoping and praying and maybe a winning lottery ticket, they think their destiny is in better hands than their own.

If we get to Mars and find intelligent life, it's going to be interesting to see whether residents there know about Jesus Christ and believe that he was God's son. It doesn't seem as if God would have limited the goodness of his power to Earth alone.

One of the most persuasive arguments I ever read in opposition to my suspicion that there is no God was in Walt Whitman's *Leaves of Grass*.

Whitman wrote ". . . and mouse is miracle enough to stagger sextillions of infidels."

Anyone has to be staggered by what appears to be intelligent order in the universe. Photosynthesis and the free-enterprise system are miracles enough to stagger me, too, but I don't accept any of the thousands of manmade Gods that every collection of people who ever existed has invented to explain them.

The flaw in looking at what we have here on Earth, whether it's a mouse or photosynthesis, and calling it "orderly" is that it's only orderly in our own minds. We have applied the word order to the status quo. It has been assumed that everything on Earth—the atmosphere, the temperature, the oxygen content of the air—was made the way it is so that man could live here. The faithful make it sound as though God planned it that way so we could survive on Earth. It has an attractive sound to it but it could be used in a freshman philosophy class as an example of a fallacy.

The planet wasn't designed for our needs. The human body developed the way it is because it adapted itself to what it found on Earth.

Voltaire was kidding about the theory that everything was created by God to make man comfortable here on earth when he said how remarkable it was that "the nose was designed as a perfect place to rest eyeglasses."

Charles Darwin's *The Origin of Species* was the beginning of the end for the charming myth about Adam and Eve. It died a lingering death over a long period of years and still shows signs of life in some conservative groups who won't be making it into the twenty-first century any time soon.

They don't give up easily. Catholics were not allowed to eat meat on Fridays when I was growing up and my college roommate, Bob Ruthman, has never forgiven his parents for making him think he was going to hell and burn forever.

Bob was out with some guys one Thursday night after a basketball game and ate a hamburger at about 12:30 A.M.—technically Friday—and worried for years about being damned forever before he finally realized it was nonsense. Catholics pretty much dropped the idea of not eating meat on Fridays in the 1940s and 1950s although some still don't. Don't ask them why. And don't ask serious Jews who are serious about being Jewish, why they won't eat a BLT.

There has always been a slow, rear-guard retreat taking place by theologians in the face of scientific evidence. The most ardent Christians are willing to concede now that the world is round because they've probably been around it.

In 1992 the Pope pardoned Galileo. The Catholic Church had persecuted and threatened him with death in the 1600s if he didn't apologize and stop saying that the earth was round and revolved around the sun instead of vice versa.

Religions have retarded progress on earth a thousand ways by encouraging people to hold on to theories that were proven to be untrue a hundred or three hundred years before.

Most people who believe the Bible as the word of God are, nonetheless, willing to concede that the world is older than the 10,000 years or so that the Bible would have them believe.

The gospels were all written years after Jesus was killed. If a good reporter for *The New York Times* or one of the network news broadcasts gets it wrong as often as reporters inevitably do, on the day the event occurs, how can we expect much accuracy in the reporting of an event that took place 35 to 75 years before they wrote about it? The reporters weren't there when it happened, never met the subject of the report or interviewed any of the witnesses. And this was back when the written word was unusual and hard to preserve.

Christ himself didn't write anything down. He died when he was in his early thirties and there's an eighteen-year period in his life when we know nothing at all about him. In the recently found "gnostic" gospels he was reported to have been seen kissing Mary Magdalene but we don't know any more about it than that.

It's impossible to apply critical, reportorial or historical, methods to the New Testament or the life of Jesus and still come out believing all of it. The Bible has a lot of good things in it but it's part myth, part legend and it's filled with contradictions and inexplicable events. You can't unravel it.

There are too many puzzles. Jesus Christ—he was known by different names in different versions of the Bible—appears to have had extraordinary attributes but if he could heal the sick and make the blind see, it's not clear why he didn't make everyone well and enable all blind people to see again. Was this a decision he made or did he have his limitations? Is there another reason?

Or is the whole thing just a story?

The sophisticated retreat in regard to contradictions and errors in the Bible, by believers pushed into a corner, is to say that believing in God is not necessarily contingent on believing in the historical accuracy of everything in the Bible.

Every family has one or more Bibles around the house but very few people have ever read more than small portions of it and no one but a relative handful of students of the Bible has read it critically and without letting any allusion get past them.

The Bible is more praised than appraised.

God seems to have the same limitations to his ability to do good work as Jesus. Why do we have so many thieves and murderers in the world? Why are innocent young children killed crossing the street? How did Hitler happen with God looking on? Look what your neighbor is doing to the neighborhood.

Why does God let so many bad things happen? Especially after so many people are always asking him nicely not to?

You wouldn't know it living in basically Christian America that there are lots of Gods other than theirs. There has never been a nation or even a small tribe that didn't have a God of some kind that they worshipped. Humans obviously feel they need one.

Every religion has its own and its believers are dismissive of the gods of any other. They don't say it out loud because it's no longer politically correct but you wouldn't find a Catholic priest or a Presbyterian minister who thought any differently about Mohammed than I think about Christ—good guy but unrelated to God.

When a Congressman from South Carolina proposes school prayer, he doesn't have in mind a Muslim, Hindu, Buddhist or even a Jewish prayer.

I've always been amused and irritated by the unyielding opinion of my childhood friend Alfie's Catholic parents had or Billy's Methodists had that they, not the Baptists over on Hamilton Street, had the true word of God. Just don't expect a Baptist to explain the difference between what he believes and what the Presbyterian or the Lutheran in the other church believes. The believers in every religion are certain they're right but about what, they are uncertain. Christians feel superior to Muslims and Muslims feel superior to Christians even though the story of how Mohammed got the true word from God isn't much different from how Moses got it.

The Bible is often unclear and the various translations it has undergone since God is said to have passed his word on to Moses has made it something it must not have been originally. Moses probably wouldn't recognize much of it if it was translated back into its original language, Hebrew, and he could sit down and read it.

To say that the Bible is "the word of God" is wishful thinking. Or wishful not thinking. It's the word of a lot of writers, almost all men as far as we know, who wrote stories and had the audacity to suggest that "the word of God" was being handed down through them.

The faithful don't like to talk much about prayer. They don't like to be asked questions. There has always been a logical difficulty with prayer. Why should people pray to a God who knows every thought and wish they have? If God knows everything, isn't it insulting to suggest he doesn't know what you want until you ask him for it? And what's all the praise for? Is God insecure and susceptible to flattery?

Do people who pray think that by thanking him profusely he'll come up with even more good things for them next time?

When people thank God, as they often do, for the airline passengers who survive a crash, what do they think about the relation God had with the passengers who *were* killed?

The Pope traditionally prays for peace every Easter and the fact that it has never had any effect whatsoever in preventing or ending a war, never deters him. What goes through the Pope's mind about being rejected all the time? Does God have it in for him?

At a football game, fans pray for their team to win.

Isn't the outcome of a game beneath the dignity of God to alter? When the fullback, who has just scored, kneels, crosses himself, and thanks God is he more apt to score again because God wants to reward him for having been thoughtful enough to publicly express his gratitude?

Almost no one and certainly not those who profess belief in a formal religion, are willing to use scientifically accepted methods to test religious beliefs or the efficacity of prayer and whoever wrote the Bible was smart enough to include a line quoting God as saying something like "Don't put me to the test." Prayer doesn't stand up to any test.

The burden of proof regarding the existence of God isn't on those who aren't certain there is one. It's on the people who *are* certain there is. I don't know that there is none any more than I know for absolute certain that there is no Loch Ness monster. Proving a negative is always impossible but skeptics don't have to do that. They aren't making any claims except that it is impossible to apply logical, reportorial or historical methods of inquiry to the New Testament or the life of Jesus and still come out believing all of it.

What believers offer as proof of God's existence is very flimsy. If you question the Bible, they quote the Bible as evidence that it's the truth.

Like everyone, I look for the things that support my opinions and my doubts and reject things that don't but there's so much good history in the Bible that it's a shame there's also so much contradictory nonsense that makes it easy to disbelieve. You don't have to believe that Jesus walked on water, brought back Lazarus from the dead or didn't have a human father, to believe that he was a good person and that some of the Bible is history.

Believing in and trying to emulate a person as good as it appears Jesus Christ was is a nice thing to do but people would be better off living by the ethical guidelines that their brains have led them to understand are the sensible rules to live by.

With love, your Father.

Dear Ellen,

Your mother and I are out here somewhere in the middle of the Atlantic and I'm either optimistic or maybe just dumb thinking a note from here will get to you any time soon. I don't see any mailboxes out there. Writing a letter is its own reward, anyway, whether anyone gets it or not.

Someone did just spot a whale. Or thought they did. I never see a whale or anything when everyone else sees it. Or say they do.

The *QE II* is cruising along at thirty-two miles an hour with about 750 other WW II veterans headed for the D-Day 50th anniversary ceremonies . . . We dock in Cherbourg and drive to the beaches. President Clinton's going to be there but I don't think he'll have to drive. I'm not much for veterans' reunions but this is special. The Cronkites and Herb Caen are on board and it's fun.

Bob Hope and his wife are around. You think it ought to be a good chance to catch up on some reading but you don't. A lot of not reading what I ought to goes on in my life.

I can't get over this ship and the implications of the physics involved in keeping it afloat and moving through the water at this incredible speed. It's as if they laid a fifty story hotel on its side, fixed it up with engines and propellers and put it in the water. It has a top speed of 40 mph.

I can understand a car on wheels going 100 mph or an airplane flying 800 mph with no resistance except wind but I can't imagine the power it takes to push this hotel through water at that speed.

Some of the guys on board were shipped to Europe in 1942 on the Queen Mary, which was a lot like this. The big deal at the time was that the Queen Mary could cross the Atlantic as a troop carrier without being accompanied by Navy cruisers to protect it. It was so fast the German U-boats couldn't stay up with it for long enough to launch their torpedoes. Incredible power. (Of all the guys I knew who died during the war, I always felt worst about the ones who were on those slow freighters taking supplies to the Russians by way of Murmansk and got sunk in the ice cold water of the North Atlantic. If they made it into a lifeboat, they froze to death before they drowned.)

There are a lot of things I don't understand about big ships. I think this has eight decks. It can't possibly stick down into the water as far as it sticks out above it so why doesn't it tip over? I guess most of the weight of the engines is below the water line.

It's a wonderfully decadent, old-world way to travel. They actually serve caviar but you have to have a lot of time and a special attitude to spend five days crossing the Atlantic. I don't have it and on this second day out, I'm ready to get off. Go out there with the whales.

There are some great D-Day veterans on board. Talking to them, I'm impressed with how normal and average-American they are. I suppose they were not really great men but on that one day, they did that one great thing.

And, of course, if they have the money to pay for this, they may not be so average American as I think.

I hate myself for it but in spite of feeling trapped and a little bored, I'm enjoying myself. I'll go look for a whale now.

PUBLICAFFAIRS is a new nonfiction publishing house and a tribute to the standards, values, and flair of three persons who have served as mentors to countless reporters, writers, editors, and book people of all kinds, including me.

I.F. STONE, proprietor of *I. F. Stone's Weekly*, combined a commitment to the First Amendment with entrepreneurial zeal and reporting skill and became one of the great independent journalists in American history. At the age of eighty, Izzy published *The Trial of Socrates*, which was a national bestseller. He wrote the book after he taught himself ancient Greek.

BENJAMIN C. BRADLEE was for nearly thirty years the charismatic editorial leader of *The Washington Post*. It was Ben who gave the *Post* the range and courage to pursue such historic issues as Watergate. He supported his reporters with a tenacity that made them fearless, and it is no accident that so many became authors of influential, best-selling books.

ROBERT L. BERNSTEIN, the chief executive of Random House for more than a quarter century, guided one of the nation's premier publishing houses. Bob was personally responsible for many books of political dissent and argument that challenged tyranny around the globe. He is also the founder and was the longtime chair of Human Rights Watch, one of the most respected human rights organizations in the world.

. . .

For fifty years, the banner of Public Affairs Press was carried by its owner Morris B. Schnapper, who published Gandhi, Nasser, Toynbee, Truman, and about 1,500 other authors. In 1983 Schnapper was described by *The Washington Post* as "a redoubtable gadfly." His legacy will endure in the books to come.

Peter Osnos, *Publisher*